THE NEW FOLGER LIBRARY SHAKESPEARE

Designed to make Shakespeare's great plays available to all readers, the New Folger Library edition of Shakespeare's plays provides accurate texts in modern spelling and punctuation, as well as scene-by-scene action summaries, full explanatory notes, many pictures clarifying Shakespeare's language, and notes recording all significant departures from the early printed versions. Each play is prefaced by a brief introduction, by a guide to reading Shakespeare's language, and by accounts of his life and theater. Each play is followed by an annotated list of further readings and by a "Modern Perspective" written by an expert on that particular play.

Barbara A. Mowat is Director of Academic Programs at the Folger Shakespeare Library, Executive Editor of *Shakespeare Quarterly,* Chair of the Folger Institute, and author of *The Dramaturgy of Shakespeare's Romances* and of essays on Shakespeare's plays and on the editing of the plays.

Paul Werstine is Professor of English at the Graduate School and at King's University College at the University of Western Ontario. He is general editor of the New Variorum Shakespeare and author of many papers and articles on the printing and editing of Shakespeare's plays.

The Folger Shakespeare Library

The Folger Shakespeare Library in Washington, D.C., a privately funded research library dedicated to Shakespeare and the civilization of early modern Europe, was founded in 1932 by Henry Clay and Emily Jordan Folger. In addition to its role as the world's preeminent Shakespeare collection and its emergence as a leading center for Renaissance studies, the Folger Library offers a wide array of cultural and educational programs and services for the general public.

EDITORS

BARBARA A. MOWAT
Director of Academic Programs
Folger Shakespeare Library

PAUL WERSTINE
Professor of English
King's University College at the University of
Western Ontario, Canada

FOLGER SHAKESPEARE LIBRARY

The Tragedy of

Romeo and Juliet

By

WILLIAM SHAKESPEARE

EDITED BY BARBARA A. MOWAT
AND PAUL WERSTINE

Simon & Schuster Paperbacks
NEW YORK LONDON TORONTO SYDNEY

Simon & Schuster Paperbacks
A Division of Simon & Schuster, Inc.
1230 Avenue of the Americas
New York, NY 10020

First Washington Square Press New Folger Trade Paperback Edition November 1999
This Simon & Schuster paperback edition March 2009

SIMON & SCHUSTER PAPERBACKS and colophon are registered trademarks of Simon & Schuster, Inc.

For information regarding special discounts for bulk purchases, please contact Simon & Schuster Special Sales at 1-866-506-1949 or business@simonandschuster.com.

The Simon & Schuster Speakers Bureau can bring authors to your live event. For more information or to book an event, contact the Simon & Schuster Speakers Bureau at 1-866-248-3049 or visit our website at www.simonspeakers.com.

Manufactured in the United States of America

20   19   18   17   16   15   14   13

ISBN-13: 978-0-7434-8280-6
ISBN-10:   0-7434-8280-8

From the Director of the Library

For over four decades, the Folger Library General Reader's Shakespeare provided accurate and accessible texts of the plays and poems to students, teachers, and millions of other interested readers. Today, in an age often impatient with the past, the passion for Shakespeare continues to grow. No author speaks more powerfully to the human condition, in all its variety, than this actor/playwright from a minor sixteenth-century English village.

Over the years vast changes have occurred in the way Shakespeare's works are edited, performed, studied, and taught. The New Folger Library Shakespeare replaces the earlier versions, bringing to bear the best and most current thinking concerning both the texts and their interpretation. Here is an edition which makes the plays and poems fully understandable for modern readers using uncompromising scholarship. Professors Barbara Mowat and Paul Werstine are uniquely qualified to produce this New Folger Shakespeare for a new generation of readers. The Library is grateful for the learning, clarity, and imagination they have brought to this ambitious project.

Werner Gundersheimer,
Director of the Folger Shakespeare Library
from 1984 to 2002

Contents

Editors' Preface

In recent years, ways of dealing with Shakespeare's texts and with the interpretation of his plays have been undergoing significant change. This edition, while retaining many of the features that have always made the Folger Shakespeare so attractive to the general reader, at the same time reflects these current ways of thinking about Shakespeare. For example, modern readers, actors, and teachers have become interested in the differences between, on the one hand, the early forms in which Shakespeare's plays were first published and, on the other hand, the forms in which editors through the centuries have presented them. In response to this interest, we have based our edition on what we consider the best early printed version of a particular play (explaining our rationale in a section called "An Introduction to This Text") and have marked our changes in the text—unobtrusively, we hope, but in such a way that the curious reader can be aware that a change has been made and can consult the "Textual Notes" to discover what appeared in the early printed version.

Current ways of looking at the plays are reflected in our brief introductions, in many of the commentary notes, in the annotated lists of "Further Reading," and especially in each play's "Modern Perspective," an essay written by an outstanding scholar who brings to the reader his or her fresh assessment of the play in the light of today's interests and concerns.

As in the Folger Library General Reader's Shakespeare, which this edition replaces, we include explanatory notes designed to help make Shakespeare's language clearer to a modern reader, and we place the notes on the page facing the texts that they explain. We also follow the earlier edition in including illustrations —of objects, of clothing, of mythological figures—from books and manuscripts in the Folger Library collection. We provide fresh accounts of the life of Shakespeare, of the publishing of his plays, and of the theaters in which his plays were performed, as well as an introduction to the text itself. We also include a section called "Reading Shakespeare's Language," in which we try to help readers learn to "break the code" of Elizabethan poetic language.

For each section of each volume, we are indebted to a host of generous experts and fellow scholars. The "Reading Shakespeare's Language" sections, for example, could not have been written had not Arthur King, of Brigham Young University, and Randal Robinson, author of *Unlocking Shakespeare's Language,* led the way in untangling Shakespearean language puzzles and shared their insights and methodologies generously with us. "Shakespeare's Life" profited by the careful reading given it by S. Schoenbaum, "Shakespeare's Theater" was read and strengthened by Andrew Gurr and John Astington, and "The Publication of Shakespeare's Plays" is indebted to the comments of Peter W. M. Blayney. We, as editors, take sole responsibility for any errors in our editions.

We are grateful to the authors of the "Modern Perspectives," to Leeds Barroll and David Bevington for their generous encouragement, to the Huntington and Newberry Libraries for fellowship support, to King's College for the grants it has provided to Paul Werstine, to the Social Sciences and Humanities Research Council of Canada, which provided him with a Research Time Stipend for 1990–91, and to the Folger Institute's Center for Shakespeare Studies for its fortuitous sponsorship of a workshop on "Shakespeare's Texts for Students and

Teachers" (funded by the National Endowment for the Humanities and led by Richard Knowles of the University of Wisconsin), a workshop from which we learned an enormous amount about what is wanted by college and high-school teachers of Shakespeare today.

Our biggest debt is to the Folger Shakespeare Library: to Werner Gundersheimer, Director of the Library, who has made possible our edition; to Jean Miller, the Library's Art Curator, who combed the Library holdings for illustrations, and to Julie Ainsworth, Head of the Photography Department, who carefully photographed them; to Peggy O'Brien, Director of Education, who gave us expert advice about the needs being expressed by Shakespeare teachers and students (and to Martha Christian and other "master teachers" who used our texts in manuscript in their classrooms); to the staff of the Academic Programs Division, especially Paul Menzer (who drafted "Further Reading" material), Mary Tonkinson, Lena Cowen Orlin, Molly Haws, and Jessica Hymowitz; and, finally, to the staff of the Library Reading Room, whose patience and support have been invaluable.

Barbara A. Mowat and Paul Werstine

Shakespeare's *Romeo and Juliet*

In *Romeo and Juliet,* Shakespeare creates a world of violence and generational conflict in which two young people fall in love and die because of that love. The story is rather extraordinary in that the normal problems faced by young lovers are here so very large. It is not simply that the families of Romeo and Juliet disapprove of the lovers' affection for each other; rather, the Montagues and the Capulets are on opposite sides in a blood feud and are trying to kill each other on the streets of Verona. Every time a member of one of the two families dies in the fight, his relatives demand the blood of his killer. Because of the feud, if Romeo is discovered with Juliet by her family, he will be killed. Once Romeo is banished, the only way that Juliet can avoid being married to someone else is to take a potion that apparently kills her, so that she is buried with the bodies of her slain relatives. In this violent, death-filled world, the movement of the story from love at first sight to the union of the lovers in death seems almost inevitable.

What is so striking about this play is that, despite its extraordinary setting (one perhaps reflecting Elizabethan attitudes about hot-blooded Italians), it has become the quintessential story of young love. Because most young lovers feel that they have to overcome giant obstacles in order to be together, because they feel that they would rather die than be kept apart, and especially because the language that Shakespeare gives his young lovers is so exquisite, allowing them to say to each other just what we would all say to a lover if we only knew how, it is easy to respond to this play as if it were about all young lovers rather than about a particular couple in a

"Two households, both alike in dignity."

From Publius Terentius Afer, *Comœdiae* (1496).

very unusual world. (When the play was rewritten in the seventeenth century as *The History and Fall of Caius Marius,* the violent setting became that of a particularly discordant period in classical Rome; when Leonard Bernstein rewrote the play as *West Side Story,* he chose the violent world of New York street gangs.)

After you have read the play, we invite you to read "A Modern Perspective" on *Romeo and Juliet,* written by Professor Gail Kern Paster of George Washington University.

Reading Shakespeare's Language

For many people today, reading Shakespeare's language can be a problem—but it is a problem that can be solved. Those who have studied Latin (or even French or German or Spanish) and those who are used to reading poetry will have little difficulty understanding the language of Shakespeare's poetic drama. Others, however, need to develop the skills of untangling unusual sentence structures and of recognizing and understanding poetic compressions, omissions, and wordplay. And even those skilled in reading unusual sentence structures may have occasional trouble with Shakespeare's words. Four hundred years of "static"—caused by changes in language and in life—intervene between his speaking and our hearing. Most of his immense vocabulary is still in use, but a few of his words are not, and, worse, some of his words now have meanings quite different from those they had in the sixteenth century. In the theater, most of these difficulties are solved for us by actors who study the language and articulate it for us so that the essential meaning is heard—or, when combined with stage action, is at least *felt*. When reading on one's own, one must do what each actor does: go over the lines (often with a dictionary close at hand) until the puzzles are solved and the lines yield up their poetry and the characters speak in words and phrases that are, suddenly, rewarding and wonderfully memorable.

Shakespeare's Words

As you begin to read the opening scenes of a play by Shakespeare, you may notice occasional unfamiliar words. Some are unfamiliar simply because we no longer use them. In the opening scenes of *Romeo and Juliet*, for example, you will find the words *misadventured* (i.e., unlucky), *an* (i.e., if), *marry* (an old oath "by the Virgin Mary," which had by Shakespeare's time become a mere interjection, like "indeed"), and *soft* (an interjection that means "hold," "enough," or "wait a minute"). Words of this kind are explained in notes to the text and will become familiar the more of Shakespeare's plays you read.

Some words are strange not because of the "static" introduced by changes in language over the past centuries but because these are words that Shakespeare uses to build a dramatic world that has its own space and time. *Romeo and Juliet*, for example, builds, in its opening scenes, a location that is characterized by specific customs and conflicts. The play creates this sense of place through references to "civil blood," to maskers, to Lammastide, to bucklers, clubs, bills, and partisans. Furthermore, *Romeo and Juliet* introduces us to a poetic language by means of which its characters shape their world. This is the language of love poetry (spread throughout Europe in the sonnets of the fourteenth-century Italian poet Petrarch), which we hear in references to "Dian's wit," to Aurora, to Petrarch himself, to "Cupid's arrow," and "Love's weak childish bow." (Professor Gail Paster's essay, "A Modern Perspective," at the back of this edition of *Romeo and Juliet*, discusses the impact that the world of Petrarchan love poetry has on the life and death of the young lovers.) These "local" references create the Verona that Juliet, Romeo, Mercutio, and their fellows and guardians inhabit; it will become increasingly familiar to you as you get further into the play.

In *Romeo and Juliet*, as in all of Shakespeare's writing, the most problematic words are those that we still use but that we use with different meanings. In the opening scenes of *Romeo and Juliet*, for example, the word *heavy* has the meaning of "sorrowful," the word *envious* is used where we would say "malicious," *sadly* where we would use "gravely" or "seriously," *his* where we would use "its," *happy* where we would say "fortunate," *cousin* where we would say "kinsman," and *still* where we would say "always." Such words will be explained in the notes to the text, but they, too, will become familiar as you continue to read Shakespeare's language.

Shakespeare's Sentences

In an English sentence, meaning is quite dependent on the place given each word. "The dog bit the boy" and "The boy bit the dog" mean very different things, even though the individual words are the same. Because English places such importance on the positions of words in sentences, on the way words are arranged, unusual arrangements can puzzle a reader. Shakespeare frequently shifts his sentences away from "normal" English arrangements—often to create the rhythm he seeks, sometimes to use a line's poetic rhythm to emphasize a particular word, sometimes to give a character his or her own speech patterns or to allow the character to speak in a special way. Again, when we attend a good performance of the play, the actors will have worked out the sentence structures and will articulate the sentences so that the meaning is clear. In reading for yourself, do as the actor does. That is, when you are puzzled by a character's speech, check to see if the words are being presented in an unusual sequence.

Look first for the placement of subject and verb. Shakespeare often places the verb before the subject (e.g., instead of "He goes" we find "Goes he"). In the opening scene of *Romeo and Juliet,* when Montague says (1.1.140) "Away from light steals home my heavy son" (instead of "my son steals home"), he is using such a construction; Benvolio does so as well when, at 1.1.110–11, he says, "In the instant *came* / The fiery *Tybalt*" and at 1.2.89–90, when he says, "At this same ancient feast of Capulet's / *Sups* the fair *Rosaline.*" Such inversions rarely cause much confusion. More problematic is Shakespeare's frequent placing of the object before the subject and verb (e.g., instead of "I hit him," we might find "Him I hit"). Sampson's line to Gregory (1.1.29), "Me they shall feel," is an example of such an inversion. Montague's "Black and portentous must this humor prove" (1.1.144) is a variant of such a construction, this time with the predicate adjectives "black and portentous" preceding the subject and verb. Paris uses a similar inversion when he says, at 1.2.4, "Of honorable reckoning are you both" (where the "normal" order would be "You are both of honorable reckoning"), as does Capulet at 1.2.26–30, when he says, "Such comfort as do lusty young men feel . . . shall you this night / Inherit at my house" (where the normal order would be "You shall inherit [i.e., receive] such comfort at my house as lusty young men do feel").

Inversions are not the only unusual sentence structures in Shakespeare's language. Often in his sentences words that would normally appear together are separated from each other. (Again, this is often done to create a particular rhythm or to stress a particular word.) Capulet's instruction to Paris to "like her most whose merit most shall be" (1.2.31) separates the subject ("merit") from its verb ("shall be"). Benvolio's lines that begin at 1.1.122: "A troubled mind drove me to walk abroad, / *Where* underneath the grove of sycamore / That westward rooteth from this city side, / So early walking *did I see your son*," interrupts the normal construction "where I did see your son" by inserting a series of phrases and inverting the subject and verb. The Nurse, in 1.3, interrupts the sequence "weaned upon that day" when she says, "And *she was weaned* (I never shall forget it) / Of all the days of the year, *upon that day*." In order to create for yourself sentences that seem more like the English of everyday speech, you may wish to rearrange the words, putting together the word clusters ("merit shall be," "where I did see," "she was weaned upon that day") and placing the remaining words in their familiar order. You will usually find that the sentences will gain in clarity but will lose their rhythm or shift their emphases. You can then see for yourself why Shakespeare chose his unusual arrangement.

Locating and rearranging words that "belong together" is especially necessary in passages that separate subjects from verbs and verbs from objects by long delaying or expanding interruptions. When the Prince, at 1.1.91–93, says to the citizens of Verona,

> *Three civil brawls* bred of an airy word
> By thee, old Capulet, and Montague,
> *Have* thrice *disturbed* the quiet of *our streets,*

he uses such an interrupted construction. Romeo uses a similar construction when he says, at 1.4.113–16, *"my mind misgives* [i.e., fears that] / *Some consequence* yet hanging in the stars / *Shall* bitterly *begin* his fearful date [i.e., its dreadful term] / With this night's revels." In some plays (*Hamlet,* for instance), long interrupted sentences play an important part in the play's language. In *Romeo and Juliet,* such constructions are rare, since the sentences in this play tend to be shorter than in most of Shakespeare's plays.

Finally, in *Romeo and Juliet,* as in other of Shakespeare's plays, sentences are sometimes complicated not because of unusual structures or interruptions but because Shakespeare omits words and parts of words that English sentences normally require. (In conversation, we, too, often omit words. We say, "Heard from him yet?" and our hearer supplies the missing "Have you.") Frequent reading of Shakespeare—and of other poets—trains us to supply such missing words. In plays written ten years or so after *Romeo and Juliet,* Shakespeare uses omissions both of verbs and of nouns to great dramatic effect. In *Romeo and Juliet* omissions are few and seem to result from the poet's wish to create regular iambic pentameter lines. At 1.1.107, for instance, Montague asks "were you by?" instead of "were you nearby?" creating a rhythmically regular line. At 1.1.121 ("Peered forth the golden window of the east"), Benvolio, by omitting the word "from" in the phrase "forth from," agains creates a regular rhythm. At 1.1.133 he omits the word "one" in the line "And gladly shunned [one] who gladly fled from me," and at 1.2.103 he omits the phrase "that of" from the lines "let there be weighed / Your lady's love against [that of] some other maid."

Shakespearean Wordplay

Shakespeare plays with language so often and so variously that entire books are written on the topic. Here we will mention only two kinds of wordplay, puns and metaphors. A pun is a play on words that have more than one meaning. The opening scene of *Romeo and Juliet* begins with a whole series of puns: *move* is used to mean "provoke" and then in its more usual sense, and *stand* is used to mean "take a stand" and "stand still," building to Gregory's conclusion that "if thou art moved, thou runnest away." In these examples, the dialogue openly reminds us that the words *move* and *stand* have more than one meaning. In other places in this scene, as throughout the play, words are used so that the second meaning is implied but not spelled out. When, to take one of hundreds of examples, at 1.4.17–18 Mercutio says to Romeo, "Borrow Cupid's wings / And soar with them above a common bound," the word *bound* has the primary meaning of "a leap," but the meaning of "a limit" is also suggested. (In the glosses to the text, puns of this sort are often indicated by numbered meanings—e.g., *bound* is glossed as "(1) leap; (2) limit.") Puns are so important in this play that a section of one very crucial scene (3.5) is built around very serious punning as Juliet, on the surface, expresses anger that Romeo has killed her cousin while, with the same words, she expresses her grief at being separated from Romeo:

JULIET
    God pardon him. I do with all my heart,
    And yet no man like he doth grieve my heart.
LADY CAPULET
    That is because the traitor murderer lives.

JULIET
> Ay, madam, from the reach of these my hands.
> Would none but I might venge my cousin's death!
>
> (3.5.87–91)

In these lines, the word *grieve*, for example, is heard by her mother as meaning "incense with anger" but it also means "afflict with longing"; the word *reach* is heard by her mother as meaning "grasp," but it also means "touch." In all of Shakespeare's plays, but especially in *Romeo and Juliet*, one must stay alert to the sounds of words and to the possibility of double meanings.

A metaphor is a play on words in which one object or idea is expressed as if it were something else, something with which it shares common features. For instance, when Romeo meets Juliet at the dance, and says, as he touches her hand (1.5.104), "If I profane with my unworthiest hand / This holy shrine," and goes on to talk about their meeting as if he were a pilgrim at the shrine of a saint, he is using metaphoric language. When he sees Juliet through her window and says, "What light through yonder window breaks?" he begins a series of metaphors in which he tries to put into words how Juliet looks to him—like the sun, like stars, like a winged messenger of heaven. Metaphors are often used when the idea being conveyed is hard to express, and the speaker is thus given language that helps to carry the idea or the feeling to his or her listener—and to the audience. In Romeo's metaphors of Juliet-as-saint and Juliet-as-light, he uses metaphors from the poetic tradition that attempt to express the overpowering feelings that come with being in love.

Implied Stage Action

Finally, in reading Shakespeare's plays you should always remember that what you are reading is a performance script. The dialogue is written to be spoken by actors who, at the same time, are moving, gesturing, picking up objects, weeping, shaking their fists. Some stage action is described in what are called "stage directions"; some is suggested within the dialogue itself. Learn to be alert to such signals as you stage the play in your imagination. When, in the first scene of *Romeo and Juliet*, Tybalt says, "What, art thou drawn among these heartless hinds? / Turn thee, Benvolio; look upon thy death," it is clear that Benvolio must earlier have drawn his sword, and Benvolio's response to Tybalt, "Put up thy sword," makes it just as clear that Tybalt has drawn his—probably just when he says "Turn thee, Benvolio." When Lady Capulet says, in 1.3, "Nurse, give leave awhile. / We must talk in secret.—Nurse, come back again," we can be sure that the Nurse begins to leave; since she soon enters into the conversation, we can be equally sure that she returns as ordered. At several places in *Romeo and Juliet*, signals to the reader are not quite so clear. When Sampson says, at 1.1.34, "My naked weapon is out," one would assume that he has drawn his sword. The dialogue that follows, though, makes it improbable that he is standing there with his sword drawn. Here a director—and you as reader—must decide just what Sampson would do as he says these lines. Equally interesting challenges are offered by the fight scene in which Mercutio is killed, reportedly "under Romeo's arm." The text leaves open several possibilities for staging that killing.

It is immensely rewarding to work carefully with Shakespeare's language so that the words, the sentences, the wordplay, and the implied stage action all become clear—as readers for the past four centuries have discovered. It may be more pleasurable to attend a good performance of a play—though not everyone has thought so. But the joy of being able to stage one of Shakespeare's plays in one's imagination, to return to passages that continue to yield further meanings (or further questions) the more one reads them—these are pleasures that, for many, rival (or at least augment) those of the performed text, and certainly make it worth considerable effort to "break the code" of Elizabethan poetic drama and let free the remarkable language that makes up a Shakespeare text.

Shakespeare's Life

Surviving documents that give us glimpses into the life of William Shakespeare show us a playwright, poet, and actor who grew up in the market town of Stratford-upon-Avon, spent his professional life in London, and returned to Stratford a wealthy landowner. He was born in April 1564, died in April 1616, and is buried inside the chancel of Holy Trinity Church in Stratford.

We wish we could know more about the life of the world's greatest dramatist. His plays and poems are testaments to his wide reading—especially to his knowledge of Virgil, Ovid, Plutarch, Holinshed's *Chronicles*, and the Bible—and to his mastery of the English language, but we can only speculate about his education. We know that the King's New School in Stratford-upon-Avon was considered excellent. The school was one of the English "grammar schools" established to educate young men, primarily in Latin grammar and literature. As in other schools of the time, students began their studies at the age of four or five in the attached "petty school," and there learned to read and write in English, studying primarily the catechism from the Book of Common Prayer. After two years in the petty school, students entered the lower form (grade) of the grammar school, where they began the serious study of Latin grammar and Latin texts that would occupy most of the remainder of their school days. (Several Latin texts that Shakespeare used repeatedly in writing his plays and poems were texts that schoolboys memorized and recited.) Latin comedies were introduced early in the lower form; in the upper form, which the boys entered at age ten or eleven, students wrote their own Latin orations and declamations, studied Latin historians and rhetoricians, and began the study of Greek using the Greek New Testament.

Since the records of the Stratford "grammar school" do not survive, we cannot prove that William Shakespeare attended the school; however, every indication (his father's position as an alderman and bailiff of Stratford, the playwright's own knowledge of the Latin classics, scenes in the plays that recall grammar-school experiences—for example, *The Merry Wives of Windsor,* 4.1) suggests that he did. We also lack generally accepted documentation about Shakespeare's life after his schooling ended and his professional life in London began. His marriage in 1582 (at age eighteen) to Anne Hathaway and the subsequent births of his daughter Susanna (1583) and the twins Judith and Hamnet (1585) are recorded, but how he supported himself and where he lived are not known. Nor do we know when and why he left Stratford for the London theatrical world, nor how he rose to be the important figure in that world that he had become by the early 1590s.

We do know that by 1592 he had achieved some

prominence in London as both an actor and a playwright. In that year was published a book by the playwright Robert Greene attacking an actor who had the audacity to write blank-verse drama and who was "in his own conceit [i.e., opinion] the only Shake-scene in a country." Since Greene's attack includes a parody of a line from one of Shakespeare's early plays, there is little doubt that it is Shakespeare to whom he refers, a "Shake-scene" who had aroused Greene's fury by successfully competing with university-educated dramatists like Greene himself. It was in 1593 that Shakespeare became a published poet. In that year he published his long narrative poem *Venus and Adonis;* in 1594, he followed it with *The Rape of Lucrece.* Both poems were dedicated to the young earl of Southampton (Henry Wriothesley), who may have become Shakespeare's patron.

It seems no coincidence that Shakespeare wrote these narrative poems at a time when the theaters were closed because of the plague, a contagious epidemic disease that devastated the population of London. When the theaters reopened in 1594, Shakespeare apparently resumed his double career of actor and playwright and began his long (and seemingly profitable) service as an acting-company shareholder. Records for December of 1594 show him to be a leading member of the Lord Chamberlain's Men. It was this company of actors, later named the King's Men, for whom he would be a principal actor, dramatist, and shareholder for the rest of his career.

So far as we can tell, that career spanned about twenty years. In the 1590s, he wrote his plays on English history as well as several comedies and at least two tragedies (*Titus Andronicus* and *Romeo and Juliet*). These histories, comedies, and tragedies are the plays credited to him in 1598 in a work, *Palladis Tamia,* that in one chapter compares English writers with "Greek, Latin, and Italian Poets." There the author, Francis Meres, claims that Shakespeare is comparable to the Latin dramatists Seneca for tragedy and Plautus for comedy, and calls him "the most excellent in both kinds for the stage." He also names him "mellifluous and honey-tongued Shakespeare": "I say," writes Meres, "that the Muses would speak with Shakespeare's fine filed phrase, if they would speak English." Since Meres also mentions Shakespeare's "sugared sonnets among his private friends," it is assumed that many of Shakespeare's sonnets (not published until 1609) were also written in the 1590s.

In 1599, Shakespeare's company built a theater for themselves across the river from London, naming it the Globe. The plays that are considered by many to be Shakespeare's major tragedies (*Hamlet, Othello, King Lear,* and *Macbeth*) were written while the company was resident in this theater, as were such comedies as *Twelfth Night* and *Measure for Measure.* Many of Shakespeare's plays were performed at court (both for Queen Elizabeth I and, after her death in 1603, for King James I), some were presented at the Inns of Court (the residences of London's legal societies), and some were doubtless performed in other towns, at the universities, and at great houses when the King's Men went on tour; otherwise, his plays from 1599 to 1608 were, so far as we know, performed only at the Globe. Between 1608 and 1612, Shakespeare wrote several plays—among them *The Winter's Tale* and *The Tempest*—presumably for the company's new indoor Blackfriars theater, though the plays seem to have been performed also at the Globe and at court. Surviving documents describe a performance of *The Winter's Tale* in 1611 at the Globe, for example, and performances of *The Tempest* in 1611 and 1613 at the royal palace of Whitehall.

Shakespeare wrote very little after 1612, the year in which he probably wrote *King Henry VIII*. (It was at a performance of *Henry VIII* in 1613 that the Globe caught fire and burned to the ground.) Sometime between 1610 and 1613 he seems to have returned to live in Stratford-upon-Avon, where he owned a large house and considerable property, and where his wife and his two daughters and their husbands lived. (His son Hamnet had died in 1596.) During his professional years in London, Shakespeare had presumably derived income from the acting company's profits as well as from his own career as an actor, from the sale of his play manuscripts to the acting company, and, after 1599, from his shares as an owner of the Globe. It was presumably that income, carefully invested in land and other property, that made him the wealthy man that surviving documents show him to have become. It is also assumed that William Shakespeare's growing wealth and reputation played some part in inclining the crown, in 1596, to grant John Shakespeare, William's father, the coat of arms that he had so long sought. William Shakespeare died in Stratford on April 23, 1616 (according to the epitaph carved under his bust in Holy Trinity Church) and was buried on April 25. Seven years after his death, his collected plays were published as *Mr. William Shakespeares Comedies, Histories, & Tragedies* (the work now known as the First Folio).

The years in which Shakespeare wrote were among the most exciting in English history. Intellectually, the discovery, translation, and printing of Greek and Roman classics were making available a set of works and worldviews that interacted complexly with Christian texts and beliefs. The result was a questioning, a vital intellectual ferment, that provided energy for the period's amazing dramatic and literary output and that fed directly into Shakespeare's plays. The Ghost in *Hamlet*, for example, is wonderfully complicated in part because he is a figure from Roman tragedy—the spirit of the dead returning to seek revenge—who at the same time inhabits a Christian hell (or purgatory); Hamlet's description of humankind reflects at one moment the Neoplatonic wonderment at mankind ("What a piece of work is a man!") and, at the next, the Christian disparagement of human sinners ("And yet, to me, what is this quintessence of dust?").

As intellectual horizons expanded, so also did geographical and cosmological horizons. New worlds— both North and South America—were explored, and in them were found human beings who lived and worshiped in ways radically different from those of Renaissance Europeans and Englishmen. The universe during these years also seemed to shift and expand. Copernicus had earlier theorized that the earth was not the center of the cosmos but revolved as a planet around the sun. Galileo's telescope, created in 1609, allowed scientists to see that Copernicus had been correct: the universe was not organized with the earth at the center, nor was it so nicely circumscribed as people had, until that time, thought. In terms of expanding horizons, the impact of these discoveries on people's beliefs—religious, scientific, and philosophical—cannot be overstated.

London, too, rapidly expanded and changed during the years (from the early 1590s to around 1610) that Shakespeare lived there. London—the center of England's government, its economy, its royal court, its overseas trade—was, during these years, becoming an exciting metropolis, drawing to it thousands of new citizens every year. Troubled by overcrowding, by poverty, by recurring epidemics of the plague, London was also a mecca for the wealthy and the aristocratic, and for those who sought advancement at court, or power in government or finance or trade. One hears in Shakespeare's plays the voices of London—the struggles for power, the fear of venereal disease, the language of buying and selling. One hears as well the voices of Stratford-upon-Avon—references to the nearby Forest of Arden, to sheep herding, to small-town gossip, to village fairs and markets. Part of the richness of Shakespeare's work is the influence felt there of the various worlds in which he lived: the world of metropolitan London, the world of small-town and rural England, the world of the theater, and the worlds of craftsmen and shepherds.

That Shakespeare inhabited such worlds we know from surviving London and Stratford documents, as well as from the evidence of the plays and poems themselves. From such records we can sketch the dramatist's life. We know from his works that he was a voracious reader. We know from legal and business documents that he was a multifaceted theater man who became a wealthy landowner. We know a bit about his family life and a fair amount about his legal and financial dealings. Most scholars today depend upon such evidence as they draw their picture of the world's greatest playwright. Such, however, has not always been the case. Until the late eighteenth century, the William Shakespeare who lived in most biographies was the creation of legend and tradition. This was the Shakespeare who was supposedly caught poaching deer at Charlecote, the estate of Sir Thomas Lucy close by Stratford; this was the Shakespeare who fled from Sir Thomas's vengeance and made his way in London by taking care of horses outside a playhouse; this was the Shakespeare who reportedly could barely read, but whose natural gifts were extraordinary, whose father was a butcher who allowed his gifted son sometimes to help in the butcher shop, where William supposedly killed calves "in a high style," making a speech for the occasion. It was this legendary William Shakespeare whose Falstaff (in *1* and *2 Henry IV*) so pleased Queen Elizabeth that she demanded a play about Falstaff in love, and demanded that it be written in fourteen days (hence the existence of *The Merry Wives of Windsor*). It was this legendary Shakespeare who reached the top of his acting career in the roles of the Ghost in *Hamlet* and old Adam in *As You Like It*—and who died of a fever contracted by drinking too hard at "a merry meeting" with the poets Michael Drayton and Ben Jonson. This legendary Shakespeare is a rambunctious, undisciplined man, as attractively "wild" as his plays were seen by earlier generations to be. Unfortunately, there is no trace of evidence to support these wonderful stories.

Perhaps in response to the disreputable Shakespeare of legend—or perhaps in response to the fragmentary and, for some, all-too-ordinary Shakespeare documented by surviving records—some people since the mid-nineteenth century have argued that William Shakespeare could not have written the plays that bear his name. These persons have put forward some dozen names as more likely authors, among them Queen Elizabeth, Sir Francis Bacon, Edward de Vere (earl of Oxford), and Christopher Marlowe. Such attempts to find what for these people is a more believable author of the plays is a tribute to the regard in which the plays are held. Unfortunately for their claims, the documents that exist that provide evidence for the facts of Shakespeare's life tie him inextricably to the body of plays and poems that bear his name. Unlikely as it seems to those who want the works to have been written by an aristocrat, a university graduate, or an "important" person, the plays and poems seem clearly to have been produced by a man from Stratford-upon-Avon with a very good "grammar school" education and a life of experience in London and in the world of the London theater. How this particular man produced the works that dominate the cultures of much of the world almost four hundred years after his death is one of life's mysteries—and one that will continue to tease our imaginations as we continue to delight in his plays and poems.

Shakespeare's Theater

The actors of Shakespeare's time are known to have performed plays in a great variety of locations. They played at court (that is, in the great halls of such royal residences as Whitehall, Hampton Court, and Greenwich); they played in halls at the universities of Oxford and Cambridge, and at the Inns of Court (the residences in London of the legal societies); and they also played in the private houses of great lords and civic officials. Sometimes acting companies went on tour from London into the provinces, often (but not only) when outbreaks of bubonic plague in the capital forced the closing of theaters to reduce the possibility of contagion in crowded audiences. In the provinces the actors usually staged their plays in churches (until around 1600) or in guildhalls. While surviving records show only a handful of occasions when actors played at inns while on tour, London inns were important playing-places up until the 1590s.

The building of theaters in London had begun only shortly before Shakespeare wrote his first plays in the 1590s. These theaters were of two kinds: outdoor or public playhouses that could accommodate large numbers of playgoers, and indoor or private theaters for much smaller audiences. What is usually regarded as the first London outdoor public playhouse was called simply the Theatre. James Burbage, the father of Richard Burbage, who was perhaps the most famous actor in Shakespeare's company, built it in 1576 in an area of the city of London called Shoreditch. Among the more famous of the other public playhouses that capitalized on the new fashion were the Curtain and the Fortune (both also built north of the city), the Rose, the Swan, the Globe, and the Hope (all located on the Bankside, a region just across the Thames south of the city of London). All these playhouses had to be built outside the jurisdiction of the city of London because many civic officials were hostile to the performance of drama and repeatedly petitioned the royal council to abolish it.

The theaters erected on the Bankside (a region under the authority of the Church of England, whose head was the monarch) shared the neighborhood with houses of prostitution and with the Paris Garden, where the blood sports of bearbaiting and bullbaiting were carried on. There may have been no clear distinction between playhouses and buildings for such sports, for we know that the Hope was used for both plays and baiting and that Philip Henslowe, owner of the Rose and, later, partner in the ownership of the Fortune, was also a partner in a monopoly on baiting. All these forms of entertainment were easily accessible to Londoners by boat across the Thames or over London Bridge.

Evidently Shakespeare's company prospered on the Bankside. They moved there in 1599. Threatened by difficulties in renewing the lease on the land where their first theater (the Theatre) had been built, Shakespeare's company took advantage of the Christmas holiday in 1598 to dismantle the Theatre and transport its timbers across the Thames to the Bankside, where, in 1599, these timbers were used in the building of the Globe. The weather in late December 1598 is recorded as having been especially harsh. It was so cold that the

Thames was "nigh [nearly] frozen," and there was heavy snow. Perhaps the weather aided Shakespeare's company in eluding their landlord, the snow hiding their activity and the freezing of the Thames allowing them to slide the timbers across to the Bankside without paying tolls for repeated trips over London Bridge. Attractive as this narrative is, it remains just as likely that the heavy snow hampered transport of the timbers in wagons through the London streets to the river. It also must be remembered that the Thames was, according to report, only "nigh frozen" and therefore as impassable as it ever was. Whatever the precise circumstances of this fascinating event in English theater history, Shakespeare's company was able to begin playing at their new Globe theater on the Bankside in 1599. After the first Globe burned down in 1613 during the staging of Shakespeare's *Henry VIII* (its thatch roof was set alight by cannon fire called for by the performance), Shakespeare's company immediately rebuilt on the same location. The second Globe seems to have been a grander structure than its predecessor. It remained in use until the beginning of the English Civil War in 1642, when Parliament officially closed the theaters. Soon thereafter it was pulled down.

The public theaters of Shakespeare's time were very different buildings from our theaters today. First of all, they were open-air playhouses. As recent excavations of the Rose and the Globe confirm, some were polygonal or roughly circular in shape; the Fortune, however, was square. The most recent estimates of their size put the diameter of these buildings at 72 feet (the Rose) to 100 feet (the Globe), but we know that they held vast audiences of two or three thousand, who must have been squeezed together quite tightly. Some of these spectators paid extra to sit or stand in the two or three levels of roofed galleries that extended, on the upper levels, all the way around the theater and surrounded an open space. In this space were the stage and, perhaps, the tiring house (what we would call dressing rooms), as well as the so-called yard. In the yard stood the spectators who chose to pay less, the ones whom Hamlet contemptuously called "groundlings." For a roof they had only the sky, and so they were exposed to all kinds of weather. They stood on a floor that was sometimes made of mortar and sometimes of ash mixed with the shells of hazelnuts. The latter provided a porous and therefore dry footing for the crowd, and the shells may have been more comfortable to stand on because they were not as hard as mortar. Availability of shells may not have been a problem if hazelnuts were a favorite food for Shakespeare's audiences to munch on as they watched his plays. Archaeologists who are today unearthing the remains of theaters from this period have discovered quantities of these nutshells on theater sites.

Unlike the yard, the stage itself was covered by a roof. Its ceiling, called "the heavens," is thought to have been elaborately painted to depict the sun, moon, stars, and planets. Just how big the stage was remains hard to determine. We have a single sketch of part of the interior of the Swan. A Dutchman named Johannes de Witt visited this theater around 1596 and sent a sketch of it back to his friend, Arend van Buchel. Because van Buchel found de Witt's letter and sketch of interest, he copied both into a book. It is van Buchel's copy, adapted, it seems, to the shape and size of the page in his book, that survives. In this sketch, the stage appears to be a large rectangular platform that thrusts far out into the yard, perhaps even as far as the center of the circle formed by the surrounding galleries. This drawing, combined with the specifications for the size of the stage in the building contract for the Fortune, has led scholars to conjecture that the stage on which Shakespeare's plays were performed must have measured approximately 43 feet in width and 27 feet in depth, a vast acting area. But the digging up of a large part of the Rose by archaeologists has provided evidence of a quite different stage design. The Rose stage was a platform tapered at the corners and much shallower than what seems to be depicted in the van Buchel sketch. Indeed, its measurements seem to be about 37.5 feet across at its widest point and only 15.5 feet deep. Because the surviving indications of stage size and design differ from each other so much, it is possible that the stages in other theaters, like the Theatre, the Curtain, and the Globe (the outdoor playhouses where we know that Shakespeare's plays were performed), were different from those at both the Swan and the Rose.

After about 1608 Shakespeare's plays were staged not only at the Globe but also at an indoor or private playhouse in Blackfriars. This theater had been constructed in 1596 by James Burbage in an upper hall of a former Dominican priory or monastic house. Although Henry VIII had dissolved all English monasteries in the 1530s (shortly after he had founded the Church of England), the area remained under church, rather than hostile civic, control. The hall that Burbage had purchased and renovated was a large one in which Parliament had once met. In the private theater that he constructed, the stage, lit by candles, was built across the narrow end of the hall, with boxes flanking it. The rest of the hall offered seating room only. Because there was no provision for standing room, the largest audience it could hold was less than a thousand, or about a quarter what the Globe could accommodate. Admission to Blackfriars was correspondingly more expensive. Instead of a penny to stand in the yard at the Globe, it cost a minimum of sixpence to get into Blackfriars. The best seats at the Globe (in the Lords' Room in the gallery above and behind the stage) cost sixpence; but the boxes flanking the stage at Blackfriars were half a crown, or six times sixpence. Some spectators who were particularly interested in displaying themselves paid even more to sit on stools on the Blackfriars stage.

Whether in the outdoor or indoor playhouses, the stages of Shakespeare's time were different from ours. They were not separated from the audience by the dropping of a curtain between acts and scenes. Therefore the playwrights of the time had to find other ways of signaling to the audience that one scene (to be imagined as occurring in one location at a given time) had ended and the next (to be imagined at perhaps a different location at a later time) had begun. The customary way used by Shakespeare and many of his contemporaries was to have everyone on stage exit at the end of one scene and have one or more different characters enter to begin the next. In a few cases, where characters remain onstage from one scene to another, the dialogue or stage action makes the change of location clear, and the characters are generally to be imagined as having moved from one place to another. For example, in *Romeo and Juliet,* Romeo and his friends remain onstage in Act 1 from scene 4 to scene 5, but they are represented as having moved between scenes from the street that leads to Capulet's house into Capulet's house itself. The new location is signaled in part by the appearance onstage of Capulet's servingmen carrying napkins, something they would not take into the streets. Playwrights had to be quite resourceful in the use of hand properties, like the napkin, or in the use of dialogue to specify where the action was taking place in their plays because, in contrast to most of today's theaters, the playhouses of Shakespeare's time did not use movable scenery to dress the stage and make the setting precise. As another consequence of this difference, however, the playwrights of Shakespeare's time did not have to specify exactly where the action of their plays was set when they did not choose to do so, and much of the action of their plays is tied to no specific place.

Usually Shakespeare's stage is referred to as a "bare stage," to distinguish it from the stages of the last two or three centuries with their elaborate sets. But the stage in Shakespeare's time was not completely bare. Philip Henslowe, owner of the Rose, lists in his inventory of stage properties a rock, three tombs, and two mossy banks. Stage directions in plays of the time also call for such things as thrones (or "states"), banquets (presumably tables with plaster replicas of food on them), and beds and tombs to be pushed onto the stage. Thus the stage often held more than the actors.

The actors did not limit their performing to the stage alone. Occasionally they went beneath the stage, as the Ghost appears to do in the first act of *Hamlet.* From there they could emerge onto the stage through a trapdoor. They could retire behind the hangings across the back of the stage (or the front of the tiring house), as, for example, the actor playing Polonius does when he hides behind the arras. Sometimes the hangings could be drawn back during a performance to "discover" one or more actors behind them. When performance required that an actor appear "above," as when Juliet is imagined to stand at the window of her chamber in the famous and misnamed "balcony scene," then the actor probably climbed the stairs to the gallery over the back of the stage and temporarily shared it with some of the spectators. The stage was also provided with ropes and winches so that actors could descend from, and reascend to, the "heavens."

Perhaps the greatest difference between dramatic performances in Shakespeare's time and ours was that in Shakespeare's England the roles of women were played by boys. (Some of these boys grew up to take male roles in their maturity.) There were no women in the acting companies, only in the audience. It had not always been so in the history of the English stage. There are records of women on English stages in the thirteenth and fourteenth centuries, two hundred years before Shakespeare's plays were performed. By the accession of James I in 1603, the queen of England and her ladies took part in entertainments at court called masques, and with the reopening of the theaters in 1660 at the restoration of Charles II, women again took their place on the public stage.

The chief competitors for the companies of adult actors such as the one to which Shakespeare belonged and for which he wrote were companies of exclusively boy actors. The competition was most intense in the early 1600s. There were then two principal children's companies: the Children of Paul's (the choirboys from St. Paul's Cathedral, whose private playhouse was near the cathedral); and the Children of the Chapel Royal (the choirboys from the monarch's private chapel, who performed at the Blackfriars theater built by Burbage in 1596, which Shakespeare's company had been stopped from using by local residents who objected to crowds). In *Hamlet* Shakespeare writes of "an aerie [nest] of children, little eyases [hawks], that cry out on the top of question and are most tyrannically clapped for 't. These are now the fashion and . . . berattle the common stages [attack the public theaters]." In the long run, the adult actors prevailed. The Children of Paul's dissolved around 1606. By about 1608 the Children of the Chapel Royal had been forced to stop playing at the Blackfriars theater, which was then taken over by the King's Men, Shakespeare's own troupe.

Acting companies and theaters of Shakespeare's time were organized in different ways. For example, Philip

Henslowe owned the Rose and leased it to companies of actors, who paid him from their takings. Henslowe would act as manager of these companies, initially paying playwrights for their plays and buying properties, recovering his outlay from the actors. Shakespeare's company, however, managed itself, with the principal actors, Shakespeare among them, having the status of "sharers" and the right to a share in the takings, as well as the responsibility for a part of the expenses. Five of the sharers themselves, Shakespeare among them, owned the Globe. As actor, as sharer in an acting company and in ownership of theaters, and as playwright, Shakespeare was about as involved in the theatrical industry as one could imagine. Although Shakespeare and his fellows prospered, their status under the law was conditional upon the protection of powerful patrons. "Common players"—those who did not have patrons or masters—were classed in the language of the law with "vagabonds and sturdy beggars." So the actors had to secure for themselves the official rank of servants of patrons. Among the patrons under whose protection Shakespeare's company worked were the lord chamberlain and, after the accession of King James in 1603, the king himself.

We are now perhaps on the verge of learning a great deal more about the theaters in which Shakespeare and his contemporaries performed—or at least of opening up new questions about them. Already about 70 percent of the Rose has been excavated, as has about 10 percent of the second Globe, the one built in 1614. It is to be hoped that soon more will be available for study. These are exciting times for students of Shakespeare's stage.

The Publication of Shakespeare's Plays

Eighteen of Shakespeare's plays found their way into print during the playwright's lifetime, but there is nothing to suggest that he took any interest in their publication. These eighteen appeared separately in editions called quartos. Their pages were not much larger than the one you are now reading, and these little books were sold unbound for a few pence. The earliest of the quartos that still survive were printed in 1594, the year that both *Titus Andronicus* and a version of the play now called *2 King Henry VI* became available. While almost every one of these early quartos displays on its title page the name of the acting company that performed the play, only about half provide the name of the playwright, Shakespeare. The first quarto edition to bear the name Shakespeare on its title page is *Love's Labor's Lost* of 1598. A few of these quartos were popular with the book-buying public of Shakespeare's lifetime; for example, quarto *Richard II* went through five editions between 1597 and 1615. But most of the quartos were far from best-sellers; *Love's Labor's Lost* (1598), for instance, was not reprinted in quarto until 1631. After Shakespeare's death, two more of his plays appeared in quarto format: *Othello* in 1622 and *The Two Noble Kinsmen,* coauthored with John Fletcher, in 1634.

In 1623, seven years after Shakespeare's death, was published *Mr. William Shakespeares Comedies, Histories, & Tragedies*. This printing offered readers in a single book thirty-six of the thirty-eight plays now thought to have been written by Shakespeare, including eighteen that had never been printed before. And it offered them in a style that was then reserved for serious literature and scholarship. The plays were arranged in double columns on pages nearly a foot high. This large page size is called "folio," as opposed to the smaller "quarto," and the 1623 volume is usually called the Shakespeare First Folio. It is reputed to have sold for the lordly price of a pound. (One copy at the Folger Library is marked fifteen shillings—that is, three-quarters of a pound.)

In a preface to the First Folio entitled "To the great Variety of Readers," two of Shakespeare's former fellow actors in the King's Men, John Heminge and Henry Condell, wrote that they themselves had collected their dead companion's plays. They suggested that they had seen his own papers: "we have scarce received from him a blot in his papers." The title page of the Folio declared that the plays within it had been printed "according to the True Original Copies." Comparing the Folio to the quartos, Heminge and Condell disparaged the quartos, advising their readers that "before you were abused with divers stolen and surreptitious copies, maimed, and deformed by the frauds and stealths of injurious impostors." Many Shakespeareans of the eighteenth and nineteenth centuries believed Heminge and Condell and regarded the Folio plays as superior to anything in the quartos.

Once we begin to examine the Folio plays in detail, it becomes less easy to take at face value the word of Heminge and Condell about the superiority of the Folio texts. For example, of the first nine plays in the Folio (one quarter of the entire collection), four were essentially reprinted from earlier quarto printings that Heminge and Condell had disparaged; and four have now been identified as printed from copies written in the hand of a professional scribe of the 1620s named Ralph Crane; the ninth, *The Comedy of Errors*, was apparently also printed from a manuscript, but one whose origin cannot be readily identified. Evidently then, eight of the first nine plays in the First Folio were not printed, in spite of what the Folio title page announces, "according to the True Originall Copies," or Shakespeare's own papers, and the source of the ninth is unknown. Since today's editors have been forced to treat Heminge and Condell's pronouncements with skepticism, they must choose whether to base their own editions upon quartos or the Folio on grounds other than Heminge and Condell's story of where the quarto and Folio versions originated.

Editors have often fashioned their own narratives to explain what lies behind the quartos and Folio. They have said that Heminge and Condell meant to criticize only a few of the early quartos, the ones that offer much shorter and sometimes quite different, often garbled, versions of plays. Among the examples of these are the 1600 quarto of *Henry V* (the Folio offers a much fuller version) or the 1603 *Hamlet* quarto (in 1604 a different, much longer form of the play got into print as a quarto). Early in this century editors speculated that these questionable texts were produced when someone in the audience took notes from the plays' dialogue during performances and then employed "hack poets" to fill out the notes. The poor results were then sold to a publisher and presented in print as Shakespeare's plays. More recently this story has given way to another in which the shorter versions are said to be recreations from memory of Shakespeare's plays by actors who wanted to stage them in the provinces but lacked manuscript copies. Most of the quartos offer much better texts than these so-called "bad quartos." Indeed, in most of the quartos we find texts that are at least equal to or better than what is printed in the Folio. Many of this century's Shakespeare enthusiasts have persuaded themselves that most of the quartos were set into type directly from Shakespeare's own papers, although there is nothing on which to base this conclusion except the desire for it to be true. Thus speculation continues about how the Shakespeare plays got to be printed. All that we have are the printed texts.

The book collector who was most successful in bringing together copies of the quartos and the First Folio was Henry Clay Folger, founder of the Folger Shakespeare Library in Washington, D.C. While it is estimated that there survive around the world only about 230 copies of the First Folio, Mr. Folger was able to acquire more than seventy-five copies, as well as a large number of fragments, for the library that bears his name. He also amassed a substantial number of quartos. For example, only fourteen copies of the First Quarto of *Love's Labor's Lost* are known to exist, and three are at the Folger Shakespeare Library. As a consequence of Mr. Folger's labors, twentieth-century scholars visiting the Folger Library have been able to learn a great deal about sixteenth- and seventeenth-century printing and, particularly, about the printing of Shakespeare's plays. And Mr. Folger did not stop at the First Folio, but collected many copies of later editions of Shakespeare, beginning with the Second Folio (1632), the Third (1663–64), and the Fourth (1685). Each of these later folios was based on its immediate predecessor and was edited anonymously. The first editor of Shakespeare whose name we know was Nicholas Rowe, whose first edition came out in 1709. Mr. Folger collected this edition and many, many more by Rowe's successors.

An Introduction to This Text

Romeo and Juliet was printed in a variety of forms between its earliest appearance in 1597 and its inclusion in the first collection of Shakespeare's plays, the First Folio of 1623.

In 1597 appeared *An Excellent conceited Tragedie of Romeo and Iuliet,* a quarto or pocket-size book that offers a version of the play markedly different from subsequent printings and from the play that most readers know. This version is only about two-thirds the length of later versions. It anticipates the language of these later versions quite closely (except for some apparent cuts) until near the end of Act 2. Then it offers a wedding scene that is radically different from the one in later texts. For the last three acts, the language of the First Quarto varies widely from that of later texts. While the plot is essentially the same, there sometimes is no sign at all of speeches found in later versions; and sometimes speeches appear in much abbreviated forms, which seem to most readers quite awkward in comparison to the fuller versions printed in 1599 and thereafter. This First Quarto has therefore been dubbed a "bad quarto."

In 1599 the Second Quarto, often called the "good quarto," was published. It was entitled *The Most Excellent and lamentable Tragedie of Romeo and Iuliet. Newly corrected, augmented, and amended.* For the most part, this Second Quarto seems to have been printed from a manuscript containing the fuller version of the play that most readers know. Yet there are also undeniable signs that the printer of the Second Quarto consulted the First Quarto. For a short stretch (1.2.55–1.3.37), the Second Quarto seems to be no more than a reprint of the First Quarto.

In 1609 a Third Quarto was reprinted from the Second.

A Fourth Quarto, undated, was reprinted from the Third. This Fourth Quarto has been dated by Professor G. W. Williams as having been printed in 1622. Its printer appears to have consulted the First Quarto for some corrections.

The First Folio version appeared in 1623. It reprinted the Third Quarto, but its printer's copy must have been annotated by someone, because the Folio departs from the Third Quarto in ways that seem beyond the capacities of mere typesetters.

Recent editors have been virtually unanimous in their selection of the Second Quarto as the basis for their editions. In the latter half of this century it has even been widely assumed that (except for occasional consultation of the First Quarto) the Second Quarto was printed from Shakespeare's own manuscript. In contrast, the First Quarto has been said to reproduce an abridged version put together from memory by actors who had roles in the play as it was performed outside London. Some editors have become so convinced of the truth of such stories about the First Quarto as to depend on it as a record of what was acted. Nevertheless, as today's scholars reexamine the narratives about the origins of the printed texts, we discover that these narratives are based either on questionable evidence or sometimes on none at all, and we become more skeptical about ever identifying how the play assumed the forms in which it came to be printed.

The present edition is based on a fresh examination of the early printed texts rather than upon any modern edition.* It offers readers the text as it was printed in the Second Quarto (except for the passage reprinted in the Second Quarto from the First; there this edition follows the First Quarto). But the present edition offers an *edition* of the Second Quarto because it prints such editorial changes and such readings from other early printed versions as are, in the editors' judgment, needed

---

*We have also consulted the computerized text of the Second Quarto provided by the Text Archive of the Oxford University Computing Centre, to which we are grateful.

to repair errors and deficiencies in the Second Quarto. Except for occasional readings and except for the single reprinted passage, this edition ignores the First Quarto because the First Quarto is, for the most part, so widely different from the Second.

For the convenience of the reader, we have modernized the punctuation and the spelling of the Second Quarto. Sometimes we go so far as to modernize certain old forms of words; for example, when *a* means "he," we change it to *he;* we change *mo* to *more,* and *ye* to *you.* But it is not our practice in editing any of the plays to modernize forms of words that sound distinctly different from modern forms. For example, when the early printed texts read *sith* or *apricocks* or *porpentine,* we have not modernized to *since, apricots, porcupine.* When the forms *an, and,* or *and if* appear instead of the modern form *if,* we have reduced *and* to *an* but have not changed any of these forms to their modern equivalent, *if.* We also modernize and, where necessary, correct passages in foreign languages, unless an error in the early printed text can be reasonably explained as a joke.

Whenever we change the wording of the Second Quarto or add anything to its stage directions, we mark the change by enclosing it in superior half-brackets (⌐ ⌐). We want our readers to be immediately aware when we have intervened. (Only when we correct an obvious typographical error in the Second Quarto does the change not get marked.) Whenever we change the Second Quarto's wording or change its punctuation so that meaning changes, we list the change in the textual notes at the back of the book, even if all we have done is fix an obvious error.

We correct or regularize a number of the proper names, as is the usual practice in editions of the play. "Mountague" becomes "Montague," for example, and the Prince's name, "Eskales," is printed as "Escalus." Although neither Lady Montague nor Lady Capulet receives the honorific title "Lady" in the early printed versions of the play, the title is traditional in editions and is consistent with the social relations of the families as these are depicted both in the play and in its source. Therefore we refer to these characters as "Lady Montague" and "Lady Capulet."

This edition differs from many earlier ones in its efforts to aid the reader in imagining the play as a performance rather than as a series of historical events. Thus stage directions are written with reference to the stage. For example, we do not describe Romeo and Juliet at their parting in Act 3 as being "at the window" (the First Quarto's stage direction) because there is unlikely to have been an actual window above Shakespeare's stage. Instead, we follow the Second Quarto and describe them simply as "aloft," i.e., in the gallery above the stage.

Whenever it is reasonably certain, in our view, that a speech is accompanied by a particular action, we provide a stage direction describing the action. (Occasional exceptions to this rule occur when the action is so obvious that to add a stage direction would insult the reader.) Stage directions for the entrance of characters in mid-scene are, with rare exceptions, placed so that they immediately precede the characters' participation in the scene, even though these entrances may appear somewhat earlier in the early printed texts. Whenever we move a stage direction, we record this change in the textual notes. Latin stage directions (e.g., *Exeunt*) are translated into English (e.g., *They exit*).

We expand the often severely abbreviated forms of names used as speech headings in early printed texts into the full names of the characters. We also regularize the speakers' names in speech headings, using only a single designation for each character, even though the early printed texts sometimes use a variety of designations. Variations in the speech headings of the early printed texts are recorded in the textual notes.

In the present edition, as well, we mark with a dash any change of address within a speech, unless a stage direction intervenes. When the *-ed* ending of a word is to be pronounced, we mark it with an accent. Like editors for the last two centuries, we print metrically linked lines in the following way:

BENVOLIO
  Good morrow, cousin.
  ROMEO   Is the day so young?

However, when there are a number of short verse-lines that can be linked in more than one way, we do not, with rare exceptions, indent any of them.

The Explanatory Notes

The notes that appear on the pages facing the text are designed to provide readers with the help they may need to enjoy the play. Whenever the meaning of a word in the text is not readily accessible in a good contemporary dictionary, we offer the meaning in a note. Sometimes we provide a note even when the relevant meaning is to be found in the dictionary but when the word has acquired since Shakespeare's time other potentially confusing meanings. In our notes, we try to offer modern synonyms for Shakespeare's words. We also try to indicate to the reader the connection between the word in the play and the modern synonym. For example, Shakespeare sometimes uses the word *head* to mean "source," but, for modern readers, there may be no connection evident between these two words. We provide the connection by explaining Shakespeare's usage as follows: "**head:** fountainhead, source." On some occasions, a whole phrase or clause needs explanation. Then we rephrase in our own words the difficult passage, and add at the end synonyms for individual words in the passage. When scholars have been unable to determine the meaning of a word or phrase, we acknowledge the uncertainty.

The Tragedy of

ROMEO
AND
JULIET

Characters in the Play

ROMEO
MONTAGUE, his father
LADY MONTAGUE, his mother
BENVOLIO, their kinsman
ABRAM, a Montague servingman
BALTHASAR, Romeo's servingman

JULIET
CAPULET, her father
LADY CAPULET, her mother
NURSE to Juliet
TYBALT, kinsman to the Capulets
PETRUCHIO, Tybalt's companion
Capulet's Cousin
SAMPSON
GREGORY } *servingmen*
PETER
Other Servingmen

ESCALUS, Prince of Verona
PARIS, the Prince's kinsman and Juliet's suitor
MERCUTIO, the Prince's kinsman and Romeo's friend
Paris' Page

FRIAR LAWRENCE
FRIAR JOHN
APOTHECARY
Three or four Citizens
Three Musicians
Three Watchmen

CHORUS

Attendants, Maskers, Torchbearers, a Boy with a drum,
Gentlemen, Gentlewomen, Tybalt's Page, Servingmen.

3

The Tragedy of

ROMEO

AND

JULIET

ACT 1

0 SD. **Chorus:** a character who addresses the audience, commenting on the action (Here this commentary is in the form of a sonnet.)

1. **dignity:** social position

3. **mutiny:** riot

4. **civil:** of citizens; also (ironically here) civilized

5–6. **From . . . life:** i.e., from the loins of these warring families were born two ill-fated lovers   **star-crossed:** thwarted by fate through the influence of the stars

7. **misadventured:** unlucky

11. **but:** except for

12. **two . . . stage:** i.e., the subject of our two-hour performance

"Two households, both alike in dignity." (Prologue .1)
From Publius Terentius Afer, *Comœdiae* (1496).

6

THE PROLOGUE

⌐Enter⌐ Chorus.

Two households, both alike in dignity
(In fair Verona, where we lay our scene),
From ancient grudge break to new mutiny,
Where civil blood makes civil hands unclean.
From forth the fatal loins of these two foes   5
A pair of star-crossed lovers take their life;
Whose misadventured piteous overthrows
Doth with their death bury their parents' strife.
The fearful passage of their death-marked love
And the continuance of their parents' rage,   10
Which, but their children's end, naught could remove,
Is now the two hours' traffic of our stage;
The which, if you with patient ears attend,
What here shall miss, our toil shall strive to mend.
                         ⌐Chorus exits.⌐

1.1 A street fight breaks out between the Montagues and the Capulets, which is broken up by the ruler of Verona, Prince Escalus. He threatens the Montagues and Capulets with death if they fight again.

A melancholy Romeo enters and is questioned by his cousin Benvolio, who learns that the cause of Romeo's sadness is unrequited love.

———————

0 SD. **bucklers:** small shields

1. **carry coals:** i.e., suffer humiliation patiently

2. **colliers:** carriers of coal

3. **an . . . draw:** if we are angry, we will draw our swords

5. **collar:** i.e., the hangman's noose

6. **moved:** provoked

12. **stand:** i.e., stand one's ground

13. **take the wall:** i.e., walk close to the wall (forcing others into the middle of the street)

15. **goes to the wall:** proverbial for "is shoved aside"

16–17. **women . . . vessels:** biblical: 1 Peter 3.7 (Here begins a series of sexual puns on "thrust," "heads," "stand," "tool," "weapon.")

20–21. **The quarrel . . . men:** i.e., the maids are not involved

22. **one:** the same

23. **civil:** gentle, humane

⌜ACT 1⌝

⌜Scene 1⌝
Enter Sampson and Gregory, with swords and bucklers,
of the house of Capulet.

SAMPSON Gregory, on my word we'll not carry coals.

GREGORY No, for then we should be colliers.

SAMPSON I mean, an we be in choler, we'll draw.

GREGORY Ay, while you live, draw your neck out of
collar.   5

SAMPSON I strike quickly, being moved.

GREGORY But thou art not quickly moved to strike.

SAMPSON A dog of the house of Montague moves me.

GREGORY To move is to stir, and to be valiant is to
stand. Therefore if thou art moved thou runn'st   10
away.

SAMPSON A dog of that house shall move me to stand. I
will take the wall of any man or maid of Montague's.

GREGORY That shows thee a weak slave, for the weak-
est goes to the wall.   15

SAMPSON 'Tis true, and therefore women, being the
weaker vessels, are ever thrust to the wall. Therefore I will push Montague's men from the wall and
thrust his maids to the wall.

GREGORY The quarrel is between our masters and us   20
their men.

SAMPSON 'Tis all one. I will show myself a tyrant.
When I have fought with the men, I will be civil
with the maids; I will cut off their heads.

9

27. **what sense:** whatever meaning

28. **They . . . sense:** i.e., the women must be the ones who feel what I do to them

32. **poor-john:** dried, salted fish, of poor quality; **tool:** sword

37. **Fear:** mistrust

38. **marry:** i.e., indeed; **fear:** am afraid of

39. **take . . . sides:** have the law on our side

42. **list:** please

43. **bite my thumb:** a gesture of defiance

A gentleman with sword and buckler. (1.1.0 SD)
From Cesare Vecellio, *Habiti antichi et moderni* (1598).

GREGORY   The heads of the maids?   25
SAMPSON   Ay, the heads of the maids, or their maidenheads. Take it in what sense thou wilt.
GREGORY   They must take it ⌐in⌐ sense that feel it.
SAMPSON   Me they shall feel while I am able to stand,
and 'tis known I am a pretty piece of flesh.   30
GREGORY   'Tis well thou art not fish; if thou hadst, thou
hadst been poor-john. Draw thy tool. Here comes
of the house of Montagues.

Enter ⌐Abram with another Servingman.⌐

SAMPSON   My naked weapon is out. Quarrel, I will back
thee.   35
GREGORY   How? Turn thy back and run?
SAMPSON   Fear me not.
GREGORY   No, marry. I fear thee!
SAMPSON   Let us take the law of our sides; let them
begin.   40
GREGORY   I will frown as I pass by, and let them take it
as they list.
SAMPSON   Nay, as they dare. I will bite my thumb at
them, which is disgrace to them if they bear it.
⌐*He bites his thumb.*⌐
ABRAM   Do you bite your thumb at us, sir?   45
SAMPSON   I do bite my thumb, sir.
ABRAM   Do you bite your thumb at us, sir?
SAMPSON, ⌐*aside to Gregory*⌐ Is the law of our side if I
say "Ay"?
GREGORY, ⌐*aside to Sampson*⌐ No.   50
SAMPSON   No, sir, I do not bite my thumb at you, sir,
but I bite my thumb, sir.
GREGORY   Do you quarrel, sir?
ABRAM   Quarrel, sir? No, sir.
SAMPSON   But if you do, sir, I am for you. I serve as   55
good a man as you.
ABRAM   No better.

64. **washing:** slashing with great force
67. **heartless hinds:** cowardly servants
70. **manage:** use
73. **Have at thee:** i.e., on guard!
73 SD. **partisans:** long-handled bladed weapons
74. **Clubs, bills:** a rallying cry to apprentices, who carried heavy staffs or **clubs**, and watchmen, who carried long-handled weapons or **bills**
76. **long sword:** heavy, old-fashioned weapon

Italian citizen in long gown. (1.1.75 SD)
From Cesare Vecellio, *Degli habiti antichi et moderni* (1590).

12

SAMPSON Well, sir.

Enter Benvolio.

GREGORY, ⌜*aside to Sampson*⌝ Say "better"; here comes
    one of my master's kinsmen.   60
SAMPSON Yes, better, sir.
ABRAM You lie.
SAMPSON Draw if you be men.—Gregory, remember
    thy washing blow.   *They fight.*
BENVOLIO Part, fools!   ⌜*Drawing his sword.*⌝   65
    Put up your swords. You know not what you do.

Enter Tybalt, ⌜drawing his sword.⌝

TYBALT
    What, art thou drawn among these heartless hinds?
    Turn thee, Benvolio; look upon thy death.
BENVOLIO
    I do but keep the peace. Put up thy sword,
    Or manage it to part these men with me.   70
TYBALT
    What, drawn and talk of peace? I hate the word
    As I hate hell, all Montagues, and thee.
    Have at thee, coward!   ⌜*They fight.*⌝

Enter three or four Citizens with clubs or partisans.

⌜CITIZENS⌝
    Clubs, bills, and partisans! Strike! Beat them down!
    Down with the Capulets! Down with the Montagues!   75

Enter old Capulet in his gown, and his Wife.

CAPULET
    What noise is this? Give me my long sword, ho!
LADY CAPULET A crutch, a crutch! Why call you for a
    sword?

Enter old Montague and his Wife.

80. **spite:** defiance

84. **Profaners . . . steel:** i.e., you who put weapons to degrading use by shedding your neighbors' blood

89. **mistempered:** (1) tempered (hardened) for bad purposes; (2) ill-tempered, angry

90. **movèd:** angry

95. **grave-beseeming:** appropriately sober

97. **Cankered . . . cankered:** rusted . . . virulent

99. **forfeit of the peace:** penalty for disturbing the peace

103. **our:** The prince uses the royal "we."

104. **common:** public

CAPULET
　My sword, I say. Old Montague is come
　And flourishes his blade in spite of me.　　　　　　80
MONTAGUE
　Thou villain Capulet!—Hold me not; let me go.
LADY MONTAGUE
　Thou shalt not stir one foot to seek a foe.

　　　　　　Enter Prince Escalus with his train.

PRINCE
　Rebellious subjects, enemies to peace,
　Profaners of this neighbor-stainèd steel—
　Will they not hear?—What ho! You men, you beasts,　85
　That quench the fire of your pernicious rage
　With purple fountains issuing from your veins:
　On pain of torture, from those bloody hands
　Throw your mistempered weapons to the ground,
　And hear the sentence of your movèd prince.　　　90
　Three civil brawls bred of an airy word
　By thee, old Capulet, and Montague,
　Have thrice disturbed the quiet of our streets
　And made Verona's ancient citizens
　Cast by their grave-beseeming ornaments　　　　95
　To wield old partisans in hands as old,
　Cankered with peace, to part your cankered hate.
　If ever you disturb our streets again,
　Your lives shall pay the forfeit of the peace.
　For this time all the rest depart away.　　　　　100
　You, Capulet, shall go along with me,
　And, Montague, come you this afternoon
　To know our farther pleasure in this case,
　To old Free-town, our common judgment-place.
　Once more, on pain of death, all men depart.　　105
　　　　　⌜*All but Montague, Lady Montague,*
　　　　　　　　　and Benvolio⌝ *exit.*

106. **set . . . new abroach:** i.e., stirred up the quarrel anew (literally, started it flowing again)

114. **Who:** i.e., the winds; **withal:** with it, i.e., with the sword

116. **on . . . part:** on one side and on the other

117. **either part:** both sides

122. **abroad:** out of doors

124. **That . . . side:** that grows on the west side of the city

126. **made:** went; **'ware:** aware

128. **affections:** desires

129–30. **Which . . . found:** i.e., which wanted most to find a place to be alone

132. **Pursued . . . his:** followed my own inclination by not questioning him about his

133. **who:** one who

MONTAGUE, ⌜*to Benvolio*⌝
  Who set this ancient quarrel new abroach?
  Speak, nephew, were you by when it began?
BENVOLIO
  Here were the servants of your adversary,
  And yours, close fighting ere I did approach.
  I drew to part them. In the instant came   110
  The fiery Tybalt with his sword prepared,
  Which, as he breathed defiance to my ears,
  He swung about his head and cut the winds
  Who, nothing hurt withal, hissed him in scorn.
  While we were interchanging thrusts and blows   115
  Came more and more and fought on part and part,
  Till the Prince came, who parted either part.
LADY MONTAGUE
  O, where is Romeo? Saw you him today?
  Right glad I am he was not at this fray.
BENVOLIO
  Madam, an hour before the worshiped sun   120
  Peered forth the golden window of the east,
  A troubled mind ⌜drove⌝ me to walk abroad,
  Where underneath the grove of sycamore
  That westward rooteth from this city side,
  So early walking did I see your son.   125
  Towards him I made, but he was 'ware of me
  And stole into the covert of the wood.
  I, measuring his affections by my own
  (Which then most sought where most might not be
    found,   130
  Being one too many by my weary self),
  Pursued my humor, not pursuing his,
  And gladly shunned who gladly fled from me.
MONTAGUE
  Many a morning hath he there been seen,
  With tears augmenting the fresh morning's dew,   135
  Adding to clouds more clouds with his deep sighs.

137. **all so soon:** just as soon
139. **Aurora:** goddess of the dawn
140. **heavy:** sorrowful
144. **humor:** state of mind
148. **importuned:** questioned (accent on second syllable)
151. **Is . . . true:** i.e., is perhaps not being true or faithful to himself
152. **close:** synonymous with **secret**
153. **sounding:** being sounded or searched into
154. **envious:** malicious
155. **he:** i.e., it; **his:** its
160. **his grievance:** the cause of his distress
161. **happy:** fortunate
162. **shrift:** confession

But all so soon as the all-cheering sun
Should in the farthest east begin to draw
The shady curtains from Aurora's bed,
Away from light steals home my heavy son   140
And private in his chamber pens himself,
Shuts up his windows, locks fair daylight out,
And makes himself an artificial night.
Black and portentous must this humor prove,
Unless good counsel may the cause remove.   145

BENVOLIO
My noble uncle, do you know the cause?

MONTAGUE
I neither know it nor can learn of him.

BENVOLIO
Have you importuned him by any means?

MONTAGUE
Both by myself and many other friends.
But he, ⌈his⌉ own affections' counselor,   150
Is to himself—I will not say how true,
But to himself so secret and so close,
So far from sounding and discovery,
As is the bud bit with an envious worm
Ere he can spread his sweet leaves to the air   155
Or dedicate his beauty to the same.
Could we but learn from whence his sorrows grow,
We would as willingly give cure as know.

Enter Romeo.

BENVOLIO
See where he comes. So please you, step aside.
I'll know his grievance or be much denied.   160

MONTAGUE
I would thou wert so happy by thy stay
To hear true shrift.—Come, madam, let's away.
              ⌈*Montague and Lady Montague*⌉ *exit.*

163. **morrow:** morning

174. **view:** appearance

175. **in proof:** in our experience of it

176. **love . . . still:** Cupid, god of love, is often pictured with his eyes blindfolded.   **still:** always

177. **his will:** his purposes

182. **create:** created

183. **vanity:** foolishness

184. **well-seeming:** attractive in appearance

186. **Still-waking:** always wakeful

189. **coz:** cousin

BENVOLIO
Good morrow, cousin.

ROMEO   Is the day so young?

BENVOLIO
But new struck nine.   165

ROMEO   Ay me, sad hours seem long.
Was that my father that went hence so fast?

BENVOLIO
It was. What sadness lengthens Romeo's hours?

ROMEO
Not having that, which, having, makes them short.

BENVOLIO   In love?   170

ROMEO   Out—

BENVOLIO   Of love?

ROMEO
Out of her favor where I am in love.

BENVOLIO
Alas that love, so gentle in his view,
Should be so tyrannous and rough in proof!   175

ROMEO
Alas that love, whose view is muffled still,
Should without eyes see pathways to his will!
Where shall we dine?—O me! What fray was here?
Yet tell me not, for I have heard it all.
Here's much to do with hate, but more with love.   180
Why then, O brawling love, O loving hate,
O anything of nothing first ⌜create!⌝
O heavy lightness, serious vanity,
Misshapen chaos of ⌜well-seeming⌝ forms,
Feather of lead, bright smoke, cold fire, sick health, 185
Still-waking sleep that is not what it is!
This love feel I, that feel no love in this.
Dost thou not laugh?

BENVOLIO   No, coz, I rather weep.

ROMEO
Good heart, at what?   190

193–95. **Griefs . . . thine:** i.e., you increase the weight of grief in my breast by adding your own griefs to it (The words "propagate," "breast," and "pressed" lend Romeo's words a sexual implication, as if the "new griefs" are bred upon his existing griefs.)

198. **Being purged:** i.e., love, being purged, is

200. **discreet:** judicious

203. **Soft:** i.e., wait

204. **An if:** if

207. **in sadness:** seriously

215. **fair mark:** target plainly in sight

217. **Dian's wit:** the wisdom of Diana, goddess of chastity, who was opposed to love and marriage

218. **proof:** i.e., well-tested armor

BENVOLIO   At thy good heart's oppression.
ROMEO   Why, such is love's transgression.
  Griefs of mine own lie heavy in my breast,
  Which thou wilt propagate to have it pressed
  With more of thine. This love that thou hast shown   195
  Doth add more grief to too much of mine own.
  Love is a smoke made with the fume of sighs;
  Being purged, a fire sparkling in lovers' eyes;
  Being vexed, a sea nourished with loving tears.
  What is it else? A madness most discreet,   200
  A choking gall, and a preserving sweet.
  Farewell, my coz.
BENVOLIO   Soft, I will go along.
  An if you leave me so, you do me wrong.
ROMEO
  Tut, I have lost myself. I am not here.   205
  This is not Romeo. He's some other where.
BENVOLIO
  Tell me in sadness, who is that you love?
ROMEO   What, shall I groan and tell thee?
BENVOLIO
  Groan? Why, no. But sadly tell me who.
ROMEO
  A sick man in sadness makes his will—   210
  A word ill urged to one that is so ill.
  In sadness, cousin, I do love a woman.
BENVOLIO
  I aimed so near when I supposed you loved.
ROMEO
  A right good markman! And she's fair I love.
BENVOLIO
  A right fair mark, fair coz, is soonest hit.   215
ROMEO
  Well in that hit you miss. She'll not be hit
  With Cupid's arrow. She hath Dian's wit,
  And, in strong proof of chastity well armed,

219. **uncharmed:** i.e., not subject to (love's) spell

224. **with . . . store:** Beauty dies when she does, and so does **beauty's store**, the reserve of beauty that has been deposited with her so that she may bestow it upon her offspring.

225. **still:** always

226. **sparing:** refusal to marry

229. **fair . . . fair:** beautiful . . . just

231. **forsworn to:** sworn not to

238. **To . . . more:** i.e., to force me to dwell even more upon her exquisite beauty

243. **a mistress:** any woman; **passing:** surpassingly

244. **but as a note:** except as a marginal note

245. **who:** i.e., Rosaline; **passed:** surpassed

247. **I'll . . . debt:** i.e., I undertake to teach you to forget or die trying to meet that obligation

Italian lady in a mask. (1.1.239)
From Cesare Vecellio, *Degli habiti antichi et moderni* (1590).

From love's weak childish bow she lives uncharmed.
She will not stay the siege of loving terms,   220
Nor bide th' encounter of assailing eyes,
Nor ope her lap to saint-seducing gold.
O, she is rich in beauty, only poor
That, when she dies, with beauty dies her store.

BENVOLIO
Then she hath sworn that she will still live chaste?   225

ROMEO
She hath, and in that sparing ⌜makes⌝ huge waste;
For beauty, starved with her severity,
Cuts beauty off from all posterity.
She is too fair, too wise, wisely too fair,
To merit bliss by making me despair.   230
She hath forsworn to love, and in that vow
Do I live dead, that live to tell it now.

BENVOLIO
Be ruled by me. Forget to think of her.

ROMEO
O, teach me how I should forget to think!

BENVOLIO
By giving liberty unto thine eyes.   235
Examine other beauties.

ROMEO   'Tis the way
To call hers, exquisite, in question more.
These happy masks that kiss fair ladies' brows,
Being black, puts us in mind they hide the fair.   240
He that is strucken blind cannot forget
The precious treasure of his eyesight lost.
Show me a mistress that is passing fair;
What doth her beauty serve but as a note
Where I may read who passed that passing fair?   245
Farewell. Thou canst not teach me to forget.

BENVOLIO
I'll pay that doctrine or else die in debt.

                                        They exit.

1.2 In conversation with Capulet, Count Paris declares his wish to marry Juliet. Capulet invites him to a party that night.

Capulet gives a servant the guest list for the party and orders him off to issue invitations. The servant cannot read the list and asks for help from Romeo and Benvolio. When they find out that Rosaline, on whom Romeo dotes, is invited to the party, they decide to go too.

---

0 SD. **County:** Count

1. **bound:** under bond to keep the peace

4. **reckoning:** reputation

7. **o'er:** over again

15. **hopeful lady of my earth:** perhaps, the only surviving child of my body, and thus my only heir **earth:** body; or, land and possessions

18. **agreed:** i.e., consenting

18–19. **within . . . voice:** i.e., I will consent to her marrying only someone she has chosen herself **fair:** favorable **according:** assenting

20. **accustomed:** customary

22–23. **and . . . more:** i.e., Capulet invites and welcomes Paris to be one more guest among the great many already invited **store:** abundance

26. **lusty:** vigorous

⌜Scene 2⌝
Enter Capulet, County Paris, and ⌜*a Servingman.*⌝

CAPULET
But Montague is bound as well as I,
In penalty alike, and 'tis not hard, I think,
For men so old as we to keep the peace.
PARIS
Of honorable reckoning are you both,
And pity 'tis you lived at odds so long.   5
But now, my lord, what say you to my suit?
CAPULET
But saying o'er what I have said before.
My child is yet a stranger in the world.
She hath not seen the change of fourteen years.
Let two more summers wither in their pride   10
Ere we may think her ripe to be a bride.
PARIS
Younger than she are happy mothers made.
CAPULET
And too soon marred are those so early made.
Earth hath swallowed all my hopes but she;
She's the hopeful lady of my earth.   15
But woo her, gentle Paris, get her heart;
My will to her consent is but a part.
And, she agreed, within her scope of choice
Lies my consent and fair according voice.
This night I hold an old accustomed feast,   20
Whereto I have invited many a guest
Such as I love; and you among the store,
One more, most welcome, makes my number more.
At my poor house look to behold this night
Earth-treading stars that make dark heaven light. 25
Such comfort as do lusty young men feel
When well-appareled April on the heel
Of limping winter treads, even such delight

29. **fennel:** herb believed to inspire passion

30. **Inherit:** receive

32–33. **Which . . . none:** i.e., when you gaze upon the women present, you may find my daughter to be merely one of the crowd

35. **sirrah:** term of address to a social inferior

41. **meddle:** busy himself; **yard:** yardstick; **last:** model of the foot

42. **pencil:** artist's paintbrush

48. **another's:** i.e., of another pain

50. **another's:** i.e., another grief's

52. **rank:** virulent

53. **Your plantain leaf:** a leaf used to staunch bleeding (**Your** is impersonal, meaning "the" or "a.")

55. **your broken shin:** a cut shin

57. **bound:** physically restrained

Among fresh fennel buds shall you this night
Inherit at my house. Hear all, all see,   30
And like her most whose merit most shall be;
Which, on more view of many, mine, being one,
May stand in number, though in reck'ning none.
Come go with me. ⌜*To Servingman, giving him a list.*⌝
                    Go, sirrah, trudge about   35
Through fair Verona, find those persons out
Whose names are written there, and to them say
My house and welcome on their pleasure stay.
                    ⌜*Capulet and Paris*⌝ *exit.*

SERVINGMAN   Find them out whose names are written
    here! It is written that the shoemaker should   40
    meddle with his yard and the tailor with his last, the
    fisher with his pencil and the painter with his nets.
    But I am sent to find those persons whose names
    are here writ, and can never find what names the
    writing person hath here writ. I must to the learned. 45
    In good time!

            Enter Benvolio and Romeo.

BENVOLIO, ⌜*to Romeo*⌝
    Tut man, one fire burns out another's burning;
    One pain is lessened by another's anguish.
    Turn giddy, and be helped by backward turning.
    One desperate grief cures with another's languish.   50
    Take thou some new infection to thy eye,
    And the rank poison of the old will die.
ROMEO
    Your plantain leaf is excellent for that.
BENVOLIO
    For what, I pray thee?
ROMEO   For your broken shin.   55
BENVOLIO   Why Romeo, art thou mad?
ROMEO
    Not mad, but bound more than a madman is,

59. **e'en:** evening (i.e., afternoon)

61. **God . . . e'en:** God give you good even

64–65. **without book:** by memorizing what you have heard

67. **Rest you merry:** i.e., good-bye

87. **crush:** i.e., drink

89. **ancient:** traditional

Shut up in prison, kept without my food,
Whipped and tormented, and—good e'en, good
   fellow.   60
SERVINGMAN   God gi' good e'en. I pray, sir, can you
   read?
ROMEO
Ay, mine own fortune in my misery.
SERVINGMAN   Perhaps you have learned it without
   book. But I pray, can you read anything you see?   65
ROMEO
Ay, if I know the letters and the language.
SERVINGMAN   You say honestly. Rest you merry.
ROMEO   Stay, fellow. I can read.   *(He reads the letter.)*
   Signior Martino and his wife and daughters,
   County Anselme and his beauteous sisters,   70
   The lady widow of Vitruvio,
   Signior Placentio and his lovely nieces,
   Mercutio and his brother Valentine,
   Mine Uncle Capulet, his wife and daughters,
   My fair niece Rosaline and Livia,   75
   Signior Valentio and his cousin Tybalt,
   Lucio and the lively Helena.
   A fair assembly. Whither should they come?
SERVINGMAN   Up.
ROMEO   Whither? To supper?   80
SERVINGMAN   To our house.
ROMEO   Whose house?
SERVINGMAN   My master's.
ROMEO
Indeed I should have asked thee that before.
SERVINGMAN   Now I'll tell you without asking. My   85
   master is the great rich Capulet, and, if you be not
   of the house of Montagues, I pray come and crush a
   cup of wine. Rest you merry.   ⌜*He exits.*⌝
BENVOLIO
At this same ancient feast of Capulet's

92. **unattainted:** impartial

97. **these:** i.e., my eyes

101. **fair:** i.e., to be beautiful

102. **poised:** weighed

103. **scales:** i.e., Romeo's eyes (**Scales** is treated as a singular noun.)

106. **scant:** scarcely

108. **mine own:** i.e., my love, Rosaline

1.3 Lady Capulet informs Juliet of Paris's marriage proposal and praises him extravagantly. Juliet says that she has not even dreamed of marrying, but that she will consider Paris as a possible husband if her parents wish her to.

---

3. **What:** an interjection, here perhaps suggesting impatience; **ladybird:** sweetheart

Scales. (1.2.103)
From Silvestro Pietrasanta, *Symbola heroica* (1682).

Sups the fair Rosaline whom thou so loves,   90
With all the admirèd beauties of Verona.
Go thither, and with unattainted eye
Compare her face with some that I shall show,
And I will make thee think thy swan a crow.

ROMEO
When the devout religion of mine eye   95
Maintains such falsehood, then turn tears to fire;
And these who, often drowned, could never die,
Transparent heretics, be burnt for liars.
One fairer than my love? The all-seeing sun
Ne'er saw her match since first the world begun.   100

BENVOLIO
Tut, you saw her fair, none else being by,
Herself poised with herself in either eye;
But in that crystal scales let there be weighed
Your lady's love against some other maid
That I will show you shining at this feast,   105
And she shall scant show well that now seems best.

ROMEO
I'll go along, no such sight to be shown,
But to rejoice in splendor of mine own.
⌜*They exit.*⌝

⌜Scene 3⌝
Enter ⌜*Lady Capulet*⌝ *and Nurse.*

LADY CAPULET
Nurse, where's my daughter? Call her forth to me.

NURSE
Now, by my maidenhead at twelve year old,
I bade her come.—What, lamb! What, ladybird!
God forbid. Where's this girl? What, Juliet!

Enter Juliet.

8. **give leave:** i.e., excuse us

10. **thou's:** thou shalt

14. **teen:** suffering

16. **Lammastide:** August 1 is Lammas Day. Lammastide (i.e., Lammas time) may refer either to that day or to the time around it. **Lammas Eve** is July 31.

17. **odd:** a few

28. **wormwood:** a bitter-tasting plant; **dug:** breast

33. **fool:** term of endearment

34. **fall out with:** become irritated with

35. **"Shake" . . . dovehouse:** i.e., the dovehouse shook with the earthquake   **quoth:** said

JULIET   How now, who calls?   5
NURSE   Your mother.
JULIET
   Madam, I am here. What is your will?
LADY CAPULET
   This is the matter.—Nurse, give leave awhile.
   We must talk in secret.—Nurse, come back again.
   I have remembered me, thou's hear our counsel.   10
   Thou knowest my daughter's of a pretty age.
NURSE
   Faith, I can tell her age unto ⌜an⌝ hour.
LADY CAPULET   She's not fourteen.
NURSE   I'll lay fourteen of my teeth (and yet, to my teen
      be it spoken, I have but four) she's not fourteen.   15
      How long is it now to Lammastide?
LADY CAPULET   A fortnight and odd days.
NURSE
   Even or odd, of all days in the year,
   Come Lammas Eve at night shall she be fourteen.
   Susan and she (God rest all Christian souls!)   20
   Were of an age. Well, Susan is with God;
   She was too good for me. But, as I said,
   On Lammas Eve at night shall she be fourteen.
   That shall she. Marry, I remember it well.
   'Tis since the earthquake now eleven years,   25
   And she was weaned (I never shall forget it)
   Of all the days of the year, upon that day.
   For I had then laid wormwood to my dug,
   Sitting in the sun under the dovehouse wall.
   My lord and you were then at Mantua.   30
   Nay, I do bear a brain. But, as I said,
   When it did taste the wormwood on the nipple
   Of my dug and felt it bitter, pretty fool,
   To see it tetchy and fall out with ⌜the⌝ dug.
   "Shake," quoth the dovehouse. 'Twas no need, I   35
      trow,

39. **high-lone:** i.e., by herself
40. **rood:** cross
42. **even:** just; **broke her brow:** cut her forehead
47. **holidam:** perhaps the Nurse's confusion of "holy dame" (Mary), and "halidom" (holiness)
53. **stinted:** quit (crying)
58. **stone:** testicle

To bid me trudge.
And since that time it is eleven years.
For then she could stand high-lone. Nay, by th'
    rood,   40
She could have run and waddled all about,
For even the day before, she broke her brow,
And then my husband (God be with his soul,
He was a merry man) took up the child.
"Yea," quoth he, "Dost thou fall upon thy face?   45
Thou wilt fall backward when thou hast more wit,
Wilt thou not, Jule?" And, by my holidam,
The pretty wretch left crying and said "Ay."
To see now how a jest shall come about!
I warrant, an I should live a thousand years,   50
I never should forget it. "Wilt thou not, Jule?"
    quoth he.
And, pretty fool, it stinted and said "Ay."

LADY CAPULET
Enough of this. I pray thee, hold thy peace.

NURSE
Yes, madam, yet I cannot choose but laugh   55
To think it should leave crying and say "Ay."
And yet, I warrant, it had upon its brow
A bump as big as a young cock'rel's stone,
A perilous knock, and it cried bitterly.
"Yea," quoth my husband. "Fall'st upon thy face?   60
Thou wilt fall backward when thou comest to age,
Wilt thou not, Jule?" It stinted and said "Ay."

JULIET
And stint thou, too, I pray thee, Nurse, say I.

NURSE
Peace. I have done. God mark thee to his grace,
Thou wast the prettiest babe that e'er I nursed.   65
An I might live to see thee married once,
I have my wish.

70. **disposition:** liking

73–74. **thy teat:** the nipple at which you nursed

78. **much . . . years:** i.e., at about the same age

82. **man of wax:** the ideal form of a man such as an artist might fashion in wax

87. **Read o'er the volume:** Here begins a very affected description of Paris as if he were a beautiful but unbound book in need of a cover (binding).

89. **married lineament:** perfectly matched feature

90. **content:** (1) pleasure (for the viewer); (2) substance (as in the contents of a book)

92. **margent:** margin, where obscure passages are explained

95. **pride:** splendid sight

LADY CAPULET
　Marry, that "marry" is the very theme
　I came to talk of.—Tell me, daughter Juliet,
　How stands your ⌈disposition⌉ to be married?　　　70
JULIET
　It is an ⌈honor⌉ that I dream not of.
NURSE
　An ⌈honor?⌉ Were not I thine only nurse,
　I would say thou hadst sucked wisdom from thy
　　teat.
LADY CAPULET
　Well, think of marriage now. Younger than you　75
　Here in Verona, ladies of esteem,
　Are made already mothers. By my count
　I was your mother much upon these years
　That you are now a maid. Thus, then, in brief:
　The valiant Paris seeks you for his love.　　　80
NURSE
　A man, young lady—lady, such a man
　As all the world—why, he's a man of wax.
LADY CAPULET
　Verona's summer hath not such a flower.
NURSE
　Nay, he's a flower, in faith, a very flower.
LADY CAPULET
　What say you? Can you love the gentleman?　　85
　This night you shall behold him at our feast.
　Read o'er the volume of young Paris' face,
　And find delight writ there with beauty's pen.
　Examine every married lineament
　And see how one another lends content,　　　90
　And what obscured in this fair volume lies
　Find written in the margent of his eyes.
　This precious book of love, this unbound lover,
　To beautify him only lacks a cover.
　The fish lives in the sea, and 'tis much pride　95

96. **fair without . . . within:** the beautiful outside to hide the beauty within

97–98. **That book . . . story:** In the opinion of many, a beautifully bound book shares the glory that belongs to the story printed on its pages.

108–9. **in extremity:** is urgent

110. **straight:** immediately

1.4 Romeo and Benvolio are going to the Capulets' party with their friend Mercutio and others, wearing the disguises customarily donned by "maskers." Romeo is anxious because of an ominous dream. Mercutio mocks him with a speech about a dream-giving queen of fairies.

---

0 SD. **Maskers:** participants in an impromptu masquerade of their own devising (They wear masks and fancy clothes, and offer to dance.)

1. **this speech:** i.e., an apology to their host for intruding

2. **on:** i.e., go forward with our masquerade

3. **The . . . prolixity:** such wordiness is out-of-date

For fair without the fair within to hide.
That book in many's eyes doth share the glory
That in gold clasps locks in the golden story.
So shall you share all that he doth possess
By having him, making yourself no less.   100
NURSE
No less? Nay, bigger. Women grow by men.
LADY CAPULET
Speak briefly. Can you like of Paris' love?
JULIET
I'll look to like, if looking liking move.
But no more deep will I endart mine eye
Than your consent gives strength to make ⌜it⌝ fly.   105

Enter ⌜*Servingman.*⌝

SERVINGMAN Madam, the guests are come, supper
    served up, you called, my young lady asked for, the
    Nurse cursed in the pantry, and everything in
    extremity. I must hence to wait. I beseech you,
    follow straight.   110
LADY CAPULET
We follow thee.   ⌜*Servingman exits.*⌝
            Juliet, the County stays.
NURSE Go, girl, seek happy nights to happy days.
                                    They exit.

⌜Scene 4⌝
*Enter Romeo, Mercutio, Benvolio, with five or six other
Maskers, Torchbearers,* ⌜*and a Boy with a drum.*⌝

ROMEO
What, shall this speech be spoke for our excuse?
Or shall we on without apology?
BENVOLIO
The date is out of such prolixity.

4–8. **We'll . . . entrance:** i.e., we will not preface our dancing with speeches given by someone dressed up as Cupid or with a timidly spoken prologue **Tartar's . . . bow:** an Oriental, lip-shaped bow (See page 48.) **without-book:** memorized

10. **measure . . . measure:** i.e., give them a dance
12. **heavy:** sad
16. **So:** i.e., that so
18. **bound:** (1) leap; (2) limit
19. **sore:** sorely, painfully
21. **bound a pitch:** i.e., leap to any height
23. **should you:** you would
28. **Prick . . . down:** i.e., wound love for wounding you and you thus defeat it (with a suggestion that "pricking" may satisfy desire and thus deflate it)
30. **for a visor:** for a face that is itself a mask
31. **cote:** observe

Cupid hoodwinked with a scarf. (1.4.4)
From Henry Peacham, *Minerua Britanna* (1612).

We'll have no Cupid hoodwinked with a scarf,
Bearing a Tartar's painted bow of lath,   5
Scaring the ladies like a crowkeeper,
⌜Nor no without-book prologue, faintly spoke
After the prompter, for our entrance.⌝
But let them measure us by what they will.
We'll measure them a measure and be gone.   10

ROMEO
Give me a torch. I am not for this ambling.
Being but heavy I will bear the light.

MERCUTIO
Nay, gentle Romeo, we must have you dance.

ROMEO
Not I, believe me. You have dancing shoes
With nimble soles. I have a soul of lead   15
So stakes me to the ground I cannot move.

MERCUTIO
You are a lover. Borrow Cupid's wings
And soar with them above a common bound.

ROMEO
I am too sore enpiercèd with his shaft
To soar with his light feathers, and so bound   20
I cannot bound a pitch above dull woe.
Under love's heavy burden do I sink.

⌜MERCUTIO⌝
And to sink in it should you burden love—
Too great oppression for a tender thing.

ROMEO
Is love a tender thing? It is too rough,   25
Too rude, too boist'rous, and it pricks like thorn.

MERCUTIO
If love be rough with you, be rough with love.
Prick love for pricking, and you beat love down.—
Give me a case to put my visage in.—
A visor for a visor. What care I   30
What curious eye doth cote deformities?
Here are the beetle brows shall blush for me.

34. **betake . . . legs:** i.e., dance

35. **wantons:** playful persons

37. **I . . . phrase:** i.e., I am the subject of the following old sayings

38. **I'll . . . on:** proverb: "He that worst may must hold the candle."

39. **The . . . done:** proverb: "When game is best it is time to leave."

40. **dun's . . . word:** proverb: "Dun's the mouse" (i.e., "Be still"), a fitting motto for a constable on night watch **dun:** gray-brown

41. **dun:** a play on **done** (with a reference to the game called "Dun the horse is in the mire")

42. **save your reverence:** a request to be excused for mentioning an indecent word, in this case "love," which, for Mercutio, is equivalent to "mire"

44. **we burn daylight:** i.e., we waste time (Romeo takes him literally and objects, presumably because it is evening. So in lines 46–47 Mercutio explains his sense: using up torchlight in delay is as wasteful as using lights in daytime.)

48. **good:** proper

49. **in that:** i.e., in our meaning; **wits:** senses

51. **wit:** wisdom

53. **tonight:** last night

BENVOLIO
Come, knock and enter, and no sooner in
But every man betake him to his legs.

ROMEO
A torch for me. Let wantons light of heart   35
Tickle the senseless rushes with their heels,
For I am proverbed with a grandsire phrase:
I'll be a candle holder and look on;
The game was ne'er so fair, and I am ⌈done.⌉

MERCUTIO
Tut, dun's the mouse, the constable's own word.   40
If thou art dun, we'll draw thee from the mire—
Or (save ⌈your⌉ reverence) love—wherein thou
    stickest
Up to the ears. Come, we burn daylight, ho!

ROMEO
Nay, that's not so.   45

MERCUTIO   I mean, sir, in delay
We waste our lights; in vain, ⌈light⌉ lights by day.
Take our good meaning, for our judgment sits
Five times in that ere once in our ⌈five⌉ wits.

ROMEO
And we mean well in going to this masque,   50
But 'tis no wit to go.

MERCUTIO   Why, may one ask?

ROMEO
I dreamt a dream tonight.

MERCUTIO   And so did I.

ROMEO
Well, what was yours?   55

MERCUTIO   That dreamers often lie.

ROMEO
In bed asleep while they do dream things true.

MERCUTIO
O, then I see Queen Mab hath been with you.

60. **agate stone:** quartz crystal set in a ring
62. **with:** by; **atomi:** minute creatures, atoms
64. **spinners:** spiders
65. **cover of:** cover made of
66. **traces:** harness straps
67. **collars:** part of the harness
68. **film:** fine thread, filament
69. **wagoner:** driver
72–74. These lines are printed by many editors between lines 63 and 64.
   73. **joiner:** cabinetmaker; **grub:** grubworm
   75. **in this state:** in this ceremonial splendor
   77. **on cur'sies:** of curtsies ("On" means "of" in lines 78 and 79 as well.); **straight:** immediately
   81. **sweetmeats:** candies or candied fruit
   83. **smelling out a suit:** i.e., finding someone who will pay him to present a petition to the king
   84. **tithe-pig:** a pig due to the church as part of one's tithe
   89. **breaches:** gaps in fortifications; **ambuscadoes:** ambushes; **Spanish blades:** swords of Toledo steel
   90. **healths:** toasts; **anon:** straightway
   91. **Drums:** i.e., dreams of drums
   94. **plats:** plaits, braids

She is the fairies' midwife, and she comes
In shape no bigger than an agate stone   60
On the forefinger of an alderman,
Drawn with a team of little ⌜atomi⌝
Over men's noses as they lie asleep.
Her wagon spokes made of long spinners' legs,
The cover of the wings of grasshoppers,   65
Her traces of the smallest spider web,
Her collars of the moonshine's wat'ry beams,
Her whip of cricket's bone, the lash of film,
Her wagoner a small gray-coated gnat,
Not half so big as a round little worm   70
Pricked from the lazy finger of a ⌜maid.⌝
Her chariot is an empty hazelnut,
Made by the joiner squirrel or old grub,
Time out o' mind the fairies' coachmakers.
And in this state she gallops night by night   75
Through lovers' brains, and then they dream of love;
On courtiers' knees, that dream on cur'sies straight;
O'er lawyers' fingers, who straight dream on fees;
O'er ladies' lips, who straight on kisses dream,
Which oft the angry Mab with blisters plagues   80
Because their ⌜breaths⌝ with sweetmeats tainted are.
Sometime she gallops o'er a courtier's nose,
And then dreams he of smelling out a suit.
And sometime comes she with a tithe-pig's tail,
Tickling a parson's nose as he lies asleep;   85
Then he dreams of another benefice.
Sometime she driveth o'er a soldier's neck,
And then dreams he of cutting foreign throats,
Of breaches, ambuscadoes, Spanish blades,
Of healths five fathom deep, and then anon   90
Drums in his ear, at which he starts and wakes
And, being thus frighted, swears a prayer or two
And sleeps again. This is that very Mab
That plats the manes of horses in the night

95. **bakes the elflocks in:** i.e., mats, tangles
96. **misfortune bodes:** i.e., the elves avenge themselves for the undoing of their work
98. **learns:** teaches
105. **vain fantasy:** insubstantial imagination
110. **his:** its
113. **misgives:** is apprehensive that
115. **his fearful date:** its dreadful term
116. **expire:** cause to end
118. **forfeit:** what must be given up by the debtor at the end of the **term** of a loan he cannot pay
120. **lusty:** lively
121. **drum:** drummer
121 SD. Even though the Maskers seem not to exit, the entrance of the Servingmen indicates that the scene changes to a room in Capulet's house.

A Tartar's bow. (1.4.5)
From Balthasar Küchler,
Repraesentatio der fürstlichen Auffzug (1611).

And bakes the ⌜elflocks⌝ in foul sluttish hairs,   95
Which once untangled much misfortune bodes.
This is the hag, when maids lie on their backs,
That presses them and learns them first to bear,
Making them women of good carriage.
This is she—   100
ROMEO   Peace, peace, Mercutio, peace.
Thou talk'st of nothing.
MERCUTIO   True, I talk of dreams,
Which are the children of an idle brain,
Begot of nothing but vain fantasy,   105
Which is as thin of substance as the air
And more inconstant than the wind, who woos
Even now the frozen bosom of the North
And, being angered, puffs away from thence,
Turning his side to the dew-dropping South.   110
BENVOLIO
This wind you talk of blows us from ourselves.
Supper is done, and we shall come too late.
ROMEO
I fear too early, for my mind misgives
Some consequence yet hanging in the stars
Shall bitterly begin his fearful date   115
With this night's revels, and expire the term
Of a despisèd life closed in my breast
By some vile forfeit of untimely death.
But he that hath the steerage of my course
Direct my ⌜sail.⌝ On, lusty gentlemen.   120
BENVOLIO   Strike, drum.
                              They march about the stage
                           and ⌜then withdraw to the side.⌝

1.5 Capulet welcomes the disguised Romeo and his friends. Romeo, watching the dance, is caught by the beauty of Juliet. Overhearing Romeo ask about her, Tybalt recognizes Romeo's voice and is enraged at Romeo's intrusion.

Romeo then meets Juliet, and they fall in love. Not until they are separated do they discover that they belong to enemy houses.

---

2. **take away:** i.e., take away the dirty dishes
7. **joint stools:** stools made of joined parts
8. **court cupboard:** sideboard; **plate:** utensils
9. **marchpane:** marzipan
16. **longer liver:** survivor (proverbial)
19. **walk a bout:** i.e., dance a round
22. **makes dainty:** coyly refuses (to dance)
23–24. **Am . . . now?:** i.e., have I hit close to home?

⌈Scene 5⌉
Servingmen come forth with napkins.

⌈FIRST⌉ SERVINGMAN   Where's Potpan that he helps not
    to take away? He shift a trencher? He scrape a
    trencher?
⌈SECOND⌉ SERVINGMAN   When good manners shall lie
    all in one or two men's hands, and they unwashed   5
    too, 'tis a foul thing.
⌈FIRST⌉ SERVINGMAN   Away with the joint stools, re-
    move the court cupboard, look to the plate.—
    Good thou, save me a piece of marchpane, and, as
    thou loves me, let the porter let in Susan Grind-   10
    stone and Nell.—Anthony and Potpan!
⌈THIRD⌉ SERVINGMAN   Ay, boy, ready.
⌈FIRST⌉ SERVINGMAN   You are looked for and called for,
    asked for and sought for, in the great chamber.
⌈THIRD⌉ SERVINGMAN   We cannot be here and there too.   15
    Cheerly, boys! Be brisk awhile, and the longer liver
    take all.   ⌈*They move aside.*⌉

Enter ⌈*Capulet and his household,*⌉ *all the guests and*
gentlewomen to ⌈*Romeo, Mercutio, Benvolio, and*⌉ *the*
                  ⌈*other*⌉ *Maskers.*

CAPULET
    Welcome, gentlemen. Ladies that have their toes
    Unplagued with corns will walk ⌈a bout⌉ with
        you.—   20
    Ah, my mistresses, which of you all
    Will now deny to dance? She that makes dainty,
    She, I'll swear, hath corns. Am I come near you
        now?—
    Welcome, gentlemen. I have seen the day   25
    That I have worn a visor and could tell
    A whispering tale in a fair lady's ear,
    Such as would please. 'Tis gone, 'tis gone, 'tis gone.

31. **A hall:** i.e., clear the hall for dancing

32. **turn . . . up:** i.e., remove the boards and trestles

35. **cousin:** kinsman

39. **By 'r Lady:** an oath, "by our Lady"

47. **ward:** one under the care of a guardian

57. **measure done:** dance ended; **her . . . stand:** where she stands

58. **rude:** roughly formed

Masked gentlemen and ladies. (1.5.38)
From Giacomo Franco, *Habiti d'huomeni* (1609).

You are welcome, gentlemen.—Come, musicians,
   play.   *Music plays and they dance.*   30
A hall, a hall, give room!—And foot it, girls.—
More light, you knaves, and turn the tables up,
And quench the fire; the room is grown too hot.—
Ah, sirrah, this unlooked-for sport comes well.—
Nay, sit, nay, sit, good cousin Capulet,   35
For you and I are past our dancing days.
How long is 't now since last yourself and I
Were in a mask?
CAPULET'S COUSIN By 'r Lady, thirty years.
CAPULET
   What, man, 'tis not so much, 'tis not so much.   40
   'Tis since the nuptial of ⌜Lucentio,⌝
   Come Pentecost as quickly as it will,
   Some five and twenty years, and then we masked.
CAPULET'S COUSIN
   'Tis more, 'tis more. His son is elder, sir.
   His son is thirty.   45
CAPULET   Will you tell me that?
   His son was but a ward two years ago.
ROMEO, ⌜*to a Servingman*⌝
   What lady's that which doth enrich the hand
   Of yonder knight?
SERVINGMAN   I know not, sir.   50
ROMEO
   O, she doth teach the torches to burn bright!
   It seems she hangs upon the cheek of night
   As a rich jewel in an Ethiop's ear—
   Beauty too rich for use, for earth too dear.
   So shows a snowy dove trooping with crows   55
   As yonder lady o'er her fellows shows.
   The measure done, I'll watch her place of stand
   And, touching hers, make blessèd my rude hand.
   Did my heart love till now? Forswear it, sight,
   For I ne'er saw true beauty till this night.   60

61. **should be:** must be
64. **antic face:** grotesque or fantastic mask
65. **fleer:** sneer; **solemnity:** festivity
70. **in spite:** out of malice
75. **portly:** stately
80. **patient:** calm
82. **fair presence:** gentle manner
83. **ill-beseeming semblance:** unsuitable way to appear
87. **goodman:** a man below the rank of gentleman; **Go to:** an expression of anger
89. **God . . . soul:** i.e., God save me

TYBALT
  This, by his voice, should be a Montague.—
  Fetch me my rapier, boy.   ⌜*Page exits.*⌝
                  What, dares the slave
  Come hither covered with an antic face
  To fleer and scorn at our solemnity?   65
  Now, by the stock and honor of my kin,
  To strike him dead I hold it not a sin.
CAPULET
  Why, how now, kinsman? Wherefore storm you so?
TYBALT
  Uncle, this is a Montague, our foe,
  A villain that is hither come in spite   70
  To scorn at our solemnity this night.
CAPULET
  Young Romeo is it?
TYBALT   'Tis he, that villain Romeo.
CAPULET
  Content thee, gentle coz. Let him alone.
  He bears him like a portly gentleman,   75
  And, to say truth, Verona brags of him
  To be a virtuous and well-governed youth.
  I would not for the wealth of all this town
  Here in my house do him disparagement.
  Therefore be patient. Take no note of him.   80
  It is my will, the which if thou respect,
  Show a fair presence and put off these frowns,
  An ill-beseeming semblance for a feast.
TYBALT
  It fits when such a villain is a guest.
  I'll not endure him.   85
CAPULET   He shall be endured.
  What, goodman boy? I say he shall. Go to.
  Am I the master here or you? Go to.
  You'll not endure him! God shall mend my soul,

91. **You . . . cock-a-hoop:** i.e., you will be reckless; **you'll . . . man:** i.e., you will take charge

94. **saucy:** insolent

97. Capulet begins to intersperse his rebuke of Tybalt with comments to his guests (**my hearts**) and servants. **princox:** insolent boy

100. **Patience perforce:** i.e., enforced calmness; **willful choler:** obstinate anger

104. The fourteen lines of dialogue that begin with line 104 have the structure and rhyme scheme of a sonnet.

109. **Which . . . this:** i.e., your hand shows seemly (**mannerly**) devotion in touching mine

111. **palmers:** pilgrims returning with palm branches from the Holy Land

116. **move:** initiate (blessings or favors)

You'll make a mutiny among my guests,   90
You will set cock-a-hoop, you'll be the man!
TYBALT
Why, uncle, 'tis a shame.
CAPULET   Go to, go to.
You are a saucy boy. Is 't so indeed?
This trick may chance to scathe you. I know what.   95
You must contrary me. Marry, 'tis time—
Well said, my hearts.—You are a princox, go.
Be quiet, or—More light, more light!—for shame,
I'll make you quiet.—What, cheerly, my hearts!
TYBALT
Patience perforce with willful choler meeting   100
Makes my flesh tremble in their different greeting.
I will withdraw, but this intrusion shall,
Now seeming sweet, convert to bitt'rest gall.
                                    He exits.
ROMEO, ⌜*taking Juliet's hand*⌝
If I profane with my unworthiest hand
This holy shrine, the gentle sin is this: 105
My lips, two blushing pilgrims, ready stand
To smooth that rough touch with a tender kiss.
JULIET
Good pilgrim, you do wrong your hand too much,
Which mannerly devotion shows in this;
For saints have hands that pilgrims' hands do touch, 110
And palm to palm is holy palmers' kiss.
ROMEO
Have not saints lips, and holy palmers too?
JULIET
Ay, pilgrim, lips that they must use in prayer.
ROMEO
O then, dear saint, let lips do what hands do.
They pray: grant thou, lest faith turn to despair.   115
JULIET
Saints do not move, though grant for prayers' sake.

117. **move not:** keep still

122. **You kiss by th' book:** perhaps, you speak as if well-read in the language of kissing

128. **withal:** with

130. **the chinks:** plenty of coin (money)

132. **dear:** costly; **foe's debt:** owed to a foe, i.e., Juliet

133. **The . . . best:** alluding to the proverb Romeo cited at 1.4.39

136. **banquet:** a light meal; or, dessert; **towards:** i.e., about to be served

140. **fay:** faith

ROMEO
  Then move not while my prayer's effect I take.
                              ⌐*He kisses her.*⌐
  Thus from my lips, by thine, my sin is purged.
JULIET
  Then have my lips the sin that they have took.
ROMEO
  Sin from my lips? O trespass sweetly urged!   120
  Give me my sin again.   ⌐*He kisses her.*⌐
JULIET   You kiss by th' book.
NURSE
  Madam, your mother craves a word with you.
                    ⌐*Juliet moves toward her mother.*⌐
ROMEO
  What is her mother?
NURSE   Marry, bachelor,   125
  Her mother is the lady of the house,
  And a good lady, and a wise and virtuous.
  I nursed her daughter that you talked withal.
  I tell you, he that can lay hold of her
  Shall have the chinks.   ⌐*Nurse moves away.*⌐ 130
ROMEO, ⌐*aside*⌐   Is she a Capulet?
  O dear account! My life is my foe's debt.
BENVOLIO
  Away, begone. The sport is at the best.
ROMEO
  Ay, so I fear. The more is my unrest.
CAPULET
  Nay, gentlemen, prepare not to be gone.   135
  We have a trifling foolish banquet towards.—
  Is it e'en so? Why then, I thank you all.
  I thank you, honest gentlemen. Good night.—
  More torches here.—Come on then, let's to bed.—
  Ah, sirrah, by my fay, it waxes late.   140
  I'll to my rest.
              ⌐*All but Juliet and the Nurse begin to exit.*⌐

JULIET
Come hither, Nurse. What is yond gentleman?
NURSE
The son and heir of old Tiberio.
JULIET
What's he that now is going out of door?
NURSE
Marry, that, I think, be young Petruchio.   145
JULIET
What's he that follows here, that would not dance?
NURSE   I know not.
JULIET
Go ask his name. ⌜*The Nurse goes.*⌝ If he be marrièd,
My grave is like to be my wedding bed.
NURSE, ⌜*returning*⌝
His name is Romeo, and a Montague,   150
The only son of your great enemy.
JULIET
My only love sprung from my only hate!
Too early seen unknown, and known too late!
Prodigious birth of love it is to me
That I must love a loathèd enemy.   155
NURSE
What's this? What's this?
JULIET   A rhyme I learned even now
Of one I danced withal.
                    One calls within "Juliet."
NURSE   Anon, anon.
Come, let's away. The strangers all are gone.   160
                    They exit.

The Tragedy of

ROMEO
AND
JULIET

ACT 2

0 SD. **Chorus:** Again the Chorus's speech is in the form of a sonnet.

2. **gapes:** desires eagerly

3. **fair:** i.e., fair one (Rosaline)

4. **matched:** compared

5. **again:** in return

6. **Alike bewitchèd:** just as bewitched as Juliet is

7. **complain:** plead for favor

8. **fearful:** frightening

9. **held:** considered; **access:** i.e., access to Juliet

10. **use:** are accustomed

13. **time means:** time (lends them) means

14. **Temp'ring . . . sweet:** mixing great difficulties (**extremities**) with great pleasure (**extreme sweet**)

2.1 Romeo finds himself so in love with Juliet that he cannot leave her. He scales a wall and enters Capulet's garden. Meanwhile Benvolio and Mercutio look for him in vain.

———

2. **earth:** body (which is **dull** [i.e., slow] because it is moving away from what attracts it, its **center**)

⌜ACT 2⌝

⌜*Enter*⌝ *Chorus.*

Now old desire doth in his deathbed lie,
And young affection gapes to be his heir.
That fair for which love groaned for and would die,
With tender Juliet ⌜matched,⌝ is now not fair.
Now Romeo is beloved and loves again,   5
Alike bewitchèd by the charm of looks,
But to his foe supposed he must complain,
And she steal love's sweet bait from fearful hooks.
Being held a foe, he may not have access
To breathe such vows as lovers use to swear,   10
And she as much in love, her means much less
To meet her new belovèd anywhere.
But passion lends them power, time means, to meet,
Temp'ring extremities with extreme sweet.
                                    ⌜*Chorus exits.*⌝

⌜Scene 1⌝
Enter Romeo alone.

ROMEO
Can I go forward when my heart is here?
Turn back, dull earth, and find thy center out.
                                    ⌜*He withdraws.*⌝

Enter Benvolio with Mercutio.

65

6. **orchard:** garden

8. **conjure:** raise up a spirit by invoking its proper name (In line 9 Mercutio tries out a variety of names for Romeo.)

10. **likeness:** form (Sighs and rhyming were traditionally associated with lovers.)

14. **gossip:** familiar acquaintance; **fair:** flattering

16. **Abraham:** i.e., old (as the biblical Abraham); or, cheating (An "Abraham man" was a confidence man.); **trim:** accurately

17. **King . . . maid:** alluding to a ballad

19. **ape:** i.e., a trained ape who plays dead

23. **demesnes:** regions

24. **in thy likeness:** in your own form

27. **raise:** conjure up in a magic **circle** (Mercutio's rather explicit sexual meaning is carried in the words "raise," "mistress' circle," "stand," and "laid.")

30. **were some spite:** would be some injury

Orchard. (2.1.6)
From Octavio Boldoni, *Theatrum temporaneum* (1636).

66

BENVOLIO
  Romeo, my cousin Romeo, Romeo!
MERCUTIO He is wise
  And, on my life, hath stol'n him home to bed.   5
BENVOLIO
  He ran this way and leapt this orchard wall.
  Call, good Mercutio.
⌐MERCUTIO⌐   Nay, I'll conjure too.
  Romeo! Humors! Madman! Passion! Lover!
  Appear thou in the likeness of a sigh.   10
  Speak but one rhyme and I am satisfied.
  Cry but "Ay me," ⌐pronounce⌐ but "love" and
      ⌐"dove."⌐
  Speak to my gossip Venus one fair word,
  One nickname for her purblind son and ⌐heir,⌐   15
  Young Abraham Cupid, he that shot so ⌐trim⌐
  When King Cophetua loved the beggar maid.—
  He heareth not, he stirreth not, he moveth not.
  The ape is dead, and I must conjure him.—
  I conjure thee by Rosaline's bright eyes,   20
  By her high forehead, and her scarlet lip,
  By her fine foot, straight leg, and quivering thigh,
  And the demesnes that there adjacent lie,
  That in thy likeness thou appear to us.
BENVOLIO
  An if he hear thee, thou wilt anger him.   25
MERCUTIO
  This cannot anger him. 'Twould anger him
  To raise a spirit in his mistress' circle
  Of some strange nature, letting it there stand
  Till she had laid it and conjured it down.
  That were some spite. My invocation   30
  Is fair and honest. In his mistress' name,
  I conjure only but to raise up him.
BENVOLIO
  Come, he hath hid himself among these trees

34. **consorted:** in league; **humorous:** moody
36. **mark:** target
37. **medlar:** a fruit, also called **open-arse** (See page 96.)
41. **pop'rin:** a pear from Poperinghe, in Flanders
42. **truckle bed:** i.e., trundle bed

2.2 From Capulet's garden Romeo overhears Juliet express her love for him. When he answers her, they acknowledge their love and their desire to be married.

———————

1. The scene now moves into Capulet's garden. Though the action is continuous, editors mark a new scene because of the change in location.
3–9. **It is . . . wear it:** In this elaborate comparison, Romeo plays first with the idea of the sun (Juliet) in a contest with the moon (equated with Diana, goddess of the moon). As the sun rises, the moon begins to look pale. The image then shifts toward Diana's role as goddess of chastity. Juliet is the **maid** of Diana as long as Juliet is a virgin.   **vestal livery:** clothing worn by Diana's maidens   **sick and green:** perhaps a reference to green-sickness, a form of anemia thought to afflict girls in puberty, making them pale

To be consorted with the humorous night.
Blind is his love and best befits the dark.   35
MERCUTIO
If love be blind, love cannot hit the mark.
Now will he sit under a medlar tree
And wish his mistress were that kind of fruit
As maids call medlars when they laugh alone.—
O Romeo, that she were, O, that she were   40
An open-⌐arse,⌐ thou a pop'rin pear.
Romeo, good night. I'll to my truckle bed;
This field-bed is too cold for me to sleep.—
Come, shall we go?
BENVOLIO   Go, then, for 'tis in vain   45
To seek him here that means not to be found.
                              ⌐*They*⌐ *exit.*

              ⌐Scene 2⌐
          ⌐*Romeo comes forward.*⌐

ROMEO
He jests at scars that never felt a wound.

          ⌐*Enter Juliet above.*⌐

But soft, what light through yonder window breaks?
It is the East, and Juliet is the sun.
Arise, fair sun, and kill the envious moon,
Who is already sick and pale with grief   5
That thou, her maid, art far more fair than she.
Be not her maid since she is envious.
Her vestal livery is but sick and green,
And none but fools do wear it. Cast it off.
It is my lady. O, it is my love!   10
O, that she knew she were!
She speaks, yet she says nothing. What of that?
Her eye discourses; I will answer it.

17. **spheres:** In Ptolemaic astronomy, the planets (here called **stars**) were carried in their orbits around the earth in crystalline spheres.

22. **stream:** issue a stream of light

33. **him:** the angel

36. **wherefore:** why

38. **be but:** only be

41. **but:** only

42. **Thou . . . Montague:** i.e., you would still be yourself even if you were not called Montague

43. **nor . . . nor:** neither . . . nor

Ptolemaic universe. (2.2.17)
From Marcus Manilius, *The sphere of . . .* (1675).

I am too bold. 'Tis not to me she speaks.
Two of the fairest stars in all the heaven,   15
Having some business, ⌜do⌝ entreat her eyes
To twinkle in their spheres till they return.
What if her eyes were there, they in her head?
The brightness of her cheek would shame those
    stars   20
As daylight doth a lamp; her eye in heaven
Would through the airy region stream so bright
That birds would sing and think it were not night.
See how she leans her cheek upon her hand.
O, that I were a glove upon that hand,   25
That I might touch that cheek!
JULIET   Ay me.
ROMEO, ⌜*aside*⌝   She speaks.
    O, speak again, bright angel, for thou art
As glorious to this night, being o'er my head,   30
As is a wingèd messenger of heaven
Unto the white-upturnèd wond'ring eyes
Of mortals that fall back to gaze on him
When he bestrides the lazy puffing clouds
And sails upon the bosom of the air.   35
JULIET
    O Romeo, Romeo, wherefore art thou Romeo?
Deny thy father and refuse thy name,
Or, if thou wilt not, be but sworn my love,
And I'll no longer be a Capulet.
ROMEO, ⌜*aside*⌝
    Shall I hear more, or shall I speak at this?   40
JULIET
    'Tis but thy name that is my enemy.
Thou art thyself, though not a Montague.
What's Montague? It is nor hand, nor foot,
Nor arm, nor face, ⌜nor any other part⌝
Belonging to a man. O, be some other name!   45
What's in a name? That which we call a rose

49. **owes:** owns

51. **for:** in return for

54. **Call me but:** only call me; **new baptized:** given a new Christian name

56. **bescreened:** i.e., concealed

57. **counsel:** secrets

66. **thee dislike:** displeases you

69. **death:** i.e., mortally dangerous

71. **o'erperch:** fly over

73. **And . . . attempt:** love dares to attempt whatever it is possible for love to do

74. **stop:** obstacle

By any other word would smell as sweet.
So Romeo would, were he not Romeo called,
Retain that dear perfection which he owes
Without that title. Romeo, doff thy name,   50
And, for thy name, which is no part of thee,
Take all myself.
ROMEO   I take thee at thy word.
Call me but love, and I'll be new baptized.
Henceforth I never will be Romeo.   55
JULIET
What man art thou that, thus bescreened in night,
So stumblest on my counsel?
ROMEO   By a name
I know not how to tell thee who I am.
My name, dear saint, is hateful to myself   60
Because it is an enemy to thee.
Had I it written, I would tear the word.
JULIET
My ears have yet not drunk a hundred words
Of thy tongue's uttering, yet I know the sound.
Art thou not Romeo, and a Montague?   65
ROMEO
Neither, fair maid, if either thee dislike.
JULIET
How camest thou hither, tell me, and wherefore?
The orchard walls are high and hard to climb,
And the place death, considering who thou art,
If any of my kinsmen find thee here.   70
ROMEO
With love's light wings did I o'erperch these walls,
For stony limits cannot hold love out,
And what love can do, that dares love attempt.
Therefore thy kinsmen are no stop to me.
JULIET
If they do see thee, they will murder thee.   75

78. **proof:** invulnerably armed
81. **but:** unless
83. **proroguèd:** deferred; **wanting of:** lacking
92. **For:** because of
93. **Fain . . . form:** I would gladly follow the proper formalities
94. **compliment:** observance of ceremony
102. **So:** so that; **else:** otherwise
103. **too fond:** too much in love
104. **havior light:** behavior immodest

ROMEO
    Alack, there lies more peril in thine eye
    Than twenty of their swords. Look thou but sweet,
    And I am proof against their enmity.
JULIET
    I would not for the world they saw thee here.
ROMEO
    I have night's cloak to hide me from their eyes,   80
    And, but thou love me, let them find me here.
    My life were better ended by their hate
    Than death proroguèd, wanting of thy love.
JULIET
    By whose direction found'st thou out this place?
ROMEO
    By love, that first did prompt me to inquire.   85
    He lent me counsel, and I lent him eyes.
    I am no pilot; yet, wert thou as far
    As that vast shore ⌜washed⌝ with the farthest sea,
    I should adventure for such merchandise.
JULIET
    Thou knowest the mask of night is on my face,   90
    Else would a maiden blush bepaint my cheek
    For that which thou hast heard me speak tonight.
    Fain would I dwell on form; fain, fain deny
    What I have spoke. But farewell compliment.
    Dost thou love me? I know thou wilt say "Ay,"   95
    And I will take thy word. Yet, if thou swear'st,
    Thou mayst prove false. At lovers' perjuries,
    They say, Jove laughs. O gentle Romeo,
    If thou dost love, pronounce it faithfully.
    Or, if thou thinkest I am too quickly won,   100
    I'll frown and be perverse and say thee nay,
    So thou wilt woo, but else not for the world.
    In truth, fair Montague, I am too fond,
    And therefore thou mayst think my ⌜havior⌝ light.
    But trust me, gentleman, I'll prove more true   105

106. **coying:** affectation of shyness; **strange:** distant, apparently reluctant

110. **light:** unchaste or frivolous

111. **discoverèd:** revealed

115. **orb:** sphere (See note to line 17.)

124. **contract:** accented on the second syllable

125. **unadvised:** ill-considered

Than those that have ⌜more⌝ coying to be strange.
I should have been more strange, I must confess,
But that thou overheard'st ere I was ware
My true-love passion. Therefore pardon me,
And not impute this yielding to light love,   110
Which the dark night hath so discoverèd.

ROMEO
Lady, by yonder blessed moon I vow,
That tips with silver all these fruit-tree tops—

JULIET
O, swear not by the moon, th' inconstant moon,
That monthly changes in her ⌜circled⌝ orb,   115
Lest that thy love prove likewise variable.

ROMEO
What shall I swear by?

JULIET   Do not swear at all.
Or, if thou wilt, swear by thy gracious self,
Which is the god of my idolatry,   120
And I'll believe thee.

ROMEO   If my heart's dear love—

JULIET
Well, do not swear. Although I joy in thee,
I have no joy of this contract tonight.
It is too rash, too unadvised, too sudden,   125
Too like the lightning, which doth cease to be
Ere one can say "It lightens." Sweet, good night.
This bud of love, by summer's ripening breath,
May prove a beauteous flower when next we meet.
Good night, good night. As sweet repose and rest   130
Come to thy heart as that within my breast.

ROMEO
O, wilt thou leave me so unsatisfied?

JULIET
What satisfaction canst thou have tonight?

ROMEO
Th' exchange of thy love's faithful vow for mine.

165. **want:** lack

166. **from:** i.e., go away from

168. **But . . . school:** i.e., but love goes away from love as schoolboys go toward school; **heavy:** gloomy

170. **tassel-gentle:** tercel-gentle, a male falcon

171. **Bondage is hoarse:** i.e., still under her father's rule, Juliet must keep her desires secret and whisper (hoarsely)

172. **Echo:** Shunned by her lover, Narcissus, the mythological Echo dwindled to a mere voice and lived in caves, condemned to repeat what others spoke.

177. **attending:** listening (French *attendre*)

179. **My dear:** This is the reading of the Fourth Quarto of 1622. The Second Quarto's "My Neece" (niece) is an obvious error, and the First Quarto's "Madame" is no better, since "Madam" is the term the Nurse, not Romeo, uses to address Juliet. Many editors use "My nyas," the term for a young hawk.

183. **year:** i.e., years

ROMEO   So thrive my soul—
JULIET   A thousand times good night.   ⌐*She exits.*⌐

ROMEO

A thousand times the worse to want thy light.   165
Love goes toward love as schoolboys from their
    books,
But love from love, toward school with heavy looks.
                                              ⌐*Going.*⌐

Enter Juliet ⌐above⌐ again.

JULIET

Hist, Romeo, hist! O, for a falc'ner's voice
To lure this tassel-gentle back again!   170
Bondage is hoarse and may not speak aloud,
Else would I tear the cave where Echo lies
And make her airy tongue more hoarse than ⌐mine⌐
With repetition of "My Romeo!"

ROMEO

It is my soul that calls upon my name.   175
How silver-sweet sound lovers' tongues by night,
Like softest music to attending ears.

JULIET

Romeo.

ROMEO   My ⌐dear.⌐

JULIET   What o'clock tomorrow   180
Shall I send to thee?

ROMEO   By the hour of nine.

JULIET

I will not fail. 'Tis twenty year till then.
I have forgot why I did call thee back.

ROMEO

Let me stand here till thou remember it.   185

JULIET

I shall forget, to have thee still stand there,
Rememb'ring how I love thy company.

191. **wanton:** a spoiled child
193. **gyves:** leg chains
195. **his:** its
201. **morrow:** morning
204. **ghostly:** spiritual; **close:** secluded
205. **hap:** good fortune

2.3   Determined to marry Juliet, Romeo hurries to Friar Lawrence. The Friar agrees to marry them, expressing the hope that the marriage may end the feud between their families.

———————

3. **fleckled:** light-splotched
4. **From forth:** out of the way of; **Titan:** the sun god (the Titan Helios) whose chariot is the sun

The sun god in his chariot. (2.3.4)
From mythographer Hyginus, *Fabularum liber* (1549).

ROMEO
  And I'll still stay, to have thee still forget,
  Forgetting any other home but this.
JULIET
  'Tis almost morning. I would have thee gone,   190
  And yet no farther than a wanton's bird,
  That lets it hop a little from his hand,
  Like a poor prisoner in his twisted gyves,
  And with a silken thread plucks it back again,
  So loving-jealous of his liberty.   195
ROMEO
  I would I were thy bird.
JULIET   Sweet, so would I.
  Yet I should kill thee with much cherishing.
  Good night, good night. Parting is such sweet
    sorrow   200
  That I shall say "Good night" till it be morrow.
                                        ⌜*She exits.*⌝
⌜ROMEO⌝
  Sleep dwell upon thine eyes, peace in thy breast.
  Would I were sleep and peace so sweet to rest.
  Hence will I to my ghostly friar's close cell,
  His help to crave, and my dear hap to tell.   205
                                        He exits.

                              ⌜Scene 3⌝
              Enter Friar ⌜*Lawrence*⌝ *alone with a basket.*

FRIAR LAWRENCE
  The gray-eyed morn smiles on the frowning night,
  ⌜Check'ring⌝ the eastern clouds with streaks of light,
  And fleckled darkness like a drunkard reels
  From forth day's path and Titan's ⌜fiery⌝ wheels.
  Now, ere the sun advance his burning eye,   5
  The day to cheer and night's dank dew to dry,

7. **osier cage:** i.e., basket made of willow twigs

10. **What . . . womb:** i.e., the grave in which she buries her dead is also her womb

11. **divers kind:** various kinds

13. **virtues:** powers

14. **None . . . some:** i.e., none is totally lacking in some powers (This idea is expanded in lines 17–18 below.)

15. **mickle:** great; **grace:** capacity to heal

18. **to the earth:** i.e., to humankind

19. **but:** i.e., but that; **strained:** perverted

20. **Revolts . . . birth:** i.e., it revolts from its nature

22. **by . . . dignified:** i.e., acquires worth through a good action

25–26. **with . . . part:** i.e., with the sense of smell enlivens every part of the body

27. **stays:** stops

29. **rude will:** violent inclinations, desires

31. **canker:** cankerworm

33. **Benedicite:** bless you (This five-syllable word is accented on the first, third, and fifth syllables.)

35. **argues:** indicates; **distempered:** disturbed

37. **his:** its

I must upfill this osier cage of ours
With baleful weeds and precious-juicèd flowers.
The earth that's nature's mother is her tomb;
What is her burying grave, that is her womb;   10
And from her womb children of divers kind
We sucking on her natural bosom find,
Many for many virtues excellent,
None but for some, and yet all different.
O, mickle is the powerful grace that lies   15
In plants, herbs, stones, and their true qualities.
For naught so vile that on the earth doth live
But to the earth some special good doth give;
Nor aught so good but, strained from that fair use,
Revolts from true birth, stumbling on abuse.   20
Virtue itself turns vice, being misapplied,
And vice sometime by action dignified.

Enter Romeo.

Within the infant rind of this weak flower
Poison hath residence and medicine power:
For this, being smelt, with that part cheers each   25
    part;
Being tasted, stays all senses with the heart.
Two such opposèd kings encamp them still
In man as well as herbs—grace and rude will;
And where the worser is predominant,   30
Full soon the canker death eats up that plant.
ROMEO
Good morrow, Father.
FRIAR LAWRENCE   Benedicite.
What early tongue so sweet saluteth me?
Young son, it argues a distempered head   35
So soon to bid "Good morrow" to thy bed.
Care keeps his watch in every old man's eye,
And, where care lodges, sleep will never lie;
But where unbruisèd youth with unstuffed brain

43. **distemp'rature:** disturbance of the mind
55. **Both our remedies:** the cure for both of us
56. **physic:** medicine
58. **My intercession . . . foe:** my petition is in aid of my enemy (Juliet) as well as of myself
59. **homely in thy drift:** straightforward in your meaning
60. **shrift:** absolution
64. **save:** except
67. **pass:** move along

Doth couch his limbs, there golden sleep doth   40
  reign.
Therefore thy earliness doth me assure
Thou art uproused with some distemp'rature,
Or, if not so, then here I hit it right:
Our Romeo hath not been in bed tonight.   45
ROMEO
That last is true. The sweeter rest was mine.
FRIAR LAWRENCE
God pardon sin! Wast thou with Rosaline?
ROMEO
With Rosaline, my ghostly Father? No.
I have forgot that name and that name's woe.
FRIAR LAWRENCE
That's my good son. But where hast thou been   50
  then?
ROMEO
I'll tell thee ere thou ask it me again.
I have been feasting with mine enemy,
Where on a sudden one hath wounded me
That's by me wounded. Both our remedies   55
Within thy help and holy physic lies.
I bear no hatred, blessèd man, for, lo,
My intercession likewise steads my foe.
FRIAR LAWRENCE
Be plain, good son, and homely in thy drift.
Riddling confession finds but riddling shrift.   60
ROMEO
Then plainly know my heart's dear love is set
On the fair daughter of rich Capulet.
As mine on hers, so hers is set on mine,
And all combined, save what thou must combine
By holy marriage. When and where and how   65
We met, we wooed, and made exchange of vow
I'll tell thee as we pass, but this I pray,
That thou consent to marry us today.

73. **deal of brine:** quantity of salt water (tears)

76. **season:** preserve; flavor

77. **The . . . clears:** i.e., the clouds of your sighs have not yet been dispersed by (this morning's) sun

83. **sentence:** truism, cliché

85. **may fall:** i.e., may be excused for acting immorally (This cliché assumes that men are morally stronger than women.)

86. **chid'st:** chided, scolded

88. **bad'st me:** bade me, told me to

91. **Her I love now:** i.e., the one I now love

95. **read by rote:** recite from memory; **spell:** read

97. **In one respect:** i.e., because of one consideration

FRIAR LAWRENCE
Holy Saint Francis, what a change is here!
Is Rosaline, that thou didst love so dear,   70
So soon forsaken? Young men's love then lies
Not truly in their hearts, but in their eyes.
Jesu Maria, what a deal of brine
Hath washed thy sallow cheeks for Rosaline!
How much salt water thrown away in waste   75
To season love, that of it doth not taste!
The sun not yet thy sighs from heaven clears,
Thy old groans yet ringing in mine ancient ears.
Lo, here upon thy cheek the stain doth sit
Of an old tear that is not washed off yet.   80
If e'er thou wast thyself, and these woes thine,
Thou and these woes were all for Rosaline.
And art thou changed? Pronounce this sentence
    then:
Women may fall when there's no strength in men.   85
ROMEO
Thou chid'st me oft for loving Rosaline.
FRIAR LAWRENCE
For doting, not for loving, pupil mine.
ROMEO
And bad'st me bury love.
FRIAR LAWRENCE   Not in a grave,
To lay one in another out to have.   90
ROMEO
I pray thee, chide me not. Her I love now
Doth grace for grace and love for love allow.
The other did not so.
FRIAR LAWRENCE   O, she knew well
Thy love did read by rote, that could not spell.   95
But come, young waverer, come, go with me.
In one respect I'll thy assistant be,
For this alliance may so happy prove
To turn your households' rancor to pure love.

100. **stand on:** i.e., insist on

2.4   Mercutio and Benvolio meet the newly enthusi-
astic Romeo in the street. Romeo defeats Mercutio in
a battle of wits. The Nurse finds Romeo, and he gives
her a message for Juliet: meet me at Friar Lawrence's
cell this afternoon, and we will there be married.

———————

1. **should:** can
3. **his man:** Romeo's servant
8. **his:** Romeo's
10. **answer it:** accept the challenge
12. **how:** i.e., by saying how
16. **pin:** bull's-eye
17. **blind . . . butt shaft:** Cupid's unbarbed arrow
20. **prince of cats:** Tybalt is the Prince of Cats in
Reynard the Fox.
21. **compliments:** i.e., fencing etiquette
22. **prick-song:** a written counterpoint to a simple
melody

ROMEO
O, let us hence. I stand on sudden haste.   100
FRIAR LAWRENCE
Wisely and slow. They stumble that run fast.

They exit.

⌜Scene 4⌝
Enter Benvolio and Mercutio.

MERCUTIO
Where the devil should this Romeo be?
Came he not home tonight?
BENVOLIO
Not to his father's. I spoke with his man.
MERCUTIO
Why, that same pale hard-hearted wench, that
    Rosaline,   5
Torments him so that he will sure run mad.
BENVOLIO
Tybalt, the kinsman to old Capulet,
Hath sent a letter to his father's house.
MERCUTIO   A challenge, on my life.
BENVOLIO   Romeo will answer it.   10
MERCUTIO   Any man that can write may answer a letter.
BENVOLIO   Nay, he will answer the letter's master, how
    he dares, being dared.
MERCUTIO   Alas, poor Romeo, he is already dead,
    stabbed with a white wench's black eye, run   15
    through the ear with a love-song, the very pin of his
    heart cleft with the blind bow-boy's butt shaft. And
    is he a man to encounter Tybalt?
⌜BENVOLIO⌝   Why, what is Tybalt?
MERCUTIO   More than prince of cats. O, he's the coura-   20
    geous captain of compliments. He fights as you sing
    prick-song, keeps time, distance, and proportion.

23. **rests:** pauses (in music and fencing); **minim:** a musical note, in ancient music the shortest

25. **first house:** i.e., best fencing school

26. **first . . . cause:** causes demanding satisfaction according to the code of dueling

27. **passado:** a step forward with a thrust; **punto reverso:** backhanded thrust; **hay:** successful thrust (*ai*, Italian for "thou hast [it]")

29–30. **affecting phantasimes:** pretentious fops

30. **new tuners of accent:** fashionable phrase-makers

31. **tall:** brave

35. **stand . . . on:** insist upon; **form:** (1) fashion; (2) bench

39. **Without his roe:** (1) without the first syllable of his name (so that nothing is left of him but a lover's sigh: "O me"); (2) without his "dear" (A **roe** is a small deer.); (3) sexually spent

41. **numbers:** verses; **Petrarch:** fourteenth-century Italian poet, who wrote sonnets to an idealized lady, Laura; **to:** in comparison to

43–44. **Dido . . . Cleopatra . . . Helen . . . Hero . . . Thisbe:** legendary and fictional romantic heroines

46–47. **French slop:** baggy trousers

47. **counterfeit:** i.e., slip (**Slip** [line 50] was a term for a counterfeit coin.)

50. **conceive:** understand

52. **strain:** act in violation of

He rests his minim rests, one, two, and the third in
your bosom—the very butcher of a silk button, a
duelist, a duelist, a gentleman of the very first house   25
of the first and second cause. Ah, the immortal
passado, the *punto reverso*, the *hay!*

BENVOLIO   The what?

MERCUTIO   The pox of such antic, lisping, affecting
⌐phantasimes,⌐ these new tuners of accent: "By   30
Jesu, a very good blade! A very tall man! A very good
whore!" Why, is not this a lamentable thing, grandsire, that we should be thus afflicted with these
strange flies, these fashion-mongers, these ⌐"pardon-me"'s,⌐ who stand so much on the new form   35
that they cannot sit at ease on the old bench? O their
bones, their bones!

Enter Romeo.

BENVOLIO   Here comes Romeo, here comes Romeo.

MERCUTIO   Without his roe, like a dried herring. O
flesh, flesh, how art thou fishified? Now is he for the   40
numbers that Petrarch flowed in. Laura to his lady
was a kitchen wench (marry, she had a better love
to berhyme her), Dido a dowdy, Cleopatra a gypsy,
Helen and Hero hildings and harlots, Thisbe a gray
eye or so, but not to the purpose.—Signior Romeo,   45
bonjour. There's a French salutation to your French
slop. You gave us the counterfeit fairly last night.

ROMEO   Good morrow to you both. What counterfeit
did I give you?

MERCUTIO   The slip, sir, the slip. Can you not conceive?   50

ROMEO   Pardon, good Mercutio, my business was
great, and in such a case as mine a man may strain
courtesy.

MERCUTIO   That's as much as to say such a case as
yours constrains a man to bow in the hams.   55

ROMEO   Meaning, to curtsy.

59. **pink:** (1) perfect example; (2) a flower; (3) a decorative eyelet on a shoe

62. **my . . . flowered:** my shoe well pinked (decorated)

67–68. **O . . . singleness:** feeble joke, unique in its weakness **solely singular:** unique (the only sole left)

71. **Switch and spurs:** Romeo calls on Mercutio to urge on his wit as if it were a horse.

71–72. **cry a match:** declare myself the winner

73. **wild-goose chase:** a race in which the rider in the lead chooses the course

76. **Was . . . goose?:** i.e., have I scored a victory over you by talking of the goose?

78. **for the goose:** as a fool

81. **sweeting:** a sweet-flavored apple

85. **cheveril:** kid leather, which stretches easily

86. **ell:** about 45 inches

MERCUTIO   Thou hast most kindly hit it.

ROMEO   A most courteous exposition.

MERCUTIO   Nay, I am the very pink of courtesy.

ROMEO   "Pink" for flower.   60

MERCUTIO   Right.

ROMEO   Why, then is my pump well flowered.

MERCUTIO   Sure wit, follow me this jest now till thou
hast worn out thy pump, that when the single sole
of it is worn, the jest may remain, after the wearing,   65
solely singular.

ROMEO   O single-soled jest, solely singular for the
singleness.

MERCUTIO   Come between us, good Benvolio. My wits
faints.   70

ROMEO   Switch and spurs, switch and spurs, or I'll cry
a match.

MERCUTIO   Nay, if our wits run the wild-goose chase, I
am done, for thou hast more of the wild goose in
one of thy wits than, I am sure, I have in my whole   75
five. Was I with you there for the goose?

ROMEO   Thou wast never with me for anything when
thou wast not there for the goose.

MERCUTIO   I will bite thee by the ear for that jest.

ROMEO   Nay, good goose, bite not.   80

MERCUTIO   Thy wit is a very bitter sweeting; it is a most
sharp sauce.

ROMEO   And is it not, then, well served into a sweet
goose?

MERCUTIO   O, here's a wit of cheveril that stretches   85
from an inch narrow to an ell broad.

ROMEO   I stretch it out for that word "broad," which
added to the goose, proves thee far and wide a
broad goose.

MERCUTIO   Why, is not this better now than groaning   90
for love? Now art thou sociable, now art thou
Romeo, now art thou what thou art, by art as well as

94. **natural:** idiot

95. **bauble:** (1) jester's baton; (2) penis (Possible sexual puns continue with the words "hole," "tale," "hair," "large," "short," "whole," "depth," and "occupy.")

97–98. **against the hair:** i.e., against my wishes

104. **goodly gear:** attractive stuff

105. **shirt and a smock:** i.e., a man and a woman (A shirt was a man's undergarment, a smock a woman's.)

112. **e'en:** i.e., afternoon

115. **dial:** clock; **prick:** point; penis

116. **Out upon you:** expression of annoyance; **What:** what sort of

119. **By my troth:** truly (a mild oath)

125. **fault:** lack

Medlars, or open-arses. (2.1.41)
From *The grete herball* (1529).   *96*

by nature. For this driveling love is like a great
natural that runs lolling up and down to hide his
bauble in a hole.   95

BENVOLIO   Stop there, stop there.

MERCUTIO   Thou desirest me to stop in my tale against
the hair.

BENVOLIO   Thou wouldst else have made thy tale large.

MERCUTIO   O, thou art deceived. I would have made it   100
short, for I was come to the whole depth of my tale
and meant indeed to occupy the argument no
longer.

Enter Nurse and her man ⌜*Peter.*⌝

ROMEO   Here's goodly gear. A sail, a sail!

MERCUTIO   Two, two—a shirt and a smock.   105

NURSE   Peter.

PETER   Anon.

NURSE   My fan, Peter.

MERCUTIO   Good Peter, to hide her face, for her fan's
the fairer face.   110

NURSE   God you good morrow, gentlemen.

MERCUTIO   God you good e'en, fair gentlewoman.

NURSE   Is it good e'en?

MERCUTIO   'Tis no less, I tell you, for the bawdy hand of
the dial is now upon the prick of noon.   115

NURSE   Out upon you! What a man are you?

ROMEO   One, gentlewoman, that God hath made, himself to mar.

NURSE   By my troth, it is well said: "for himself to
mar," quoth he? Gentlemen, can any of you tell me   120
where I may find the young Romeo?

ROMEO   I can tell you, but young Romeo will be older
when you have found him than he was when you
sought him. I am the youngest of that name, for
fault of a worse.   125

NURSE   You say well.

127. **took:** understood

129. **confidence:** Nurse's mistake for "conference"

131. **indite:** a deliberate "mistake" for "invite"

132. **bawd:** procuress (The word also had the dialect meaning "hare."); **So ho:** hunter's cry

134–35. **Lenten pie:** one that should contain no meat

135. **something:** somewhat; **hoar:** musty (with a pun on "whore"); **ere it be spent:** before it's used up

140. **for a score:** i.e., to pay for

141. **hoars:** turns moldy, hoary

147. **saucy merchant:** insolent fellow

148. **ropery:** perhaps, indecent talk (Mercutio's puns); or, perhaps, roguery

151. **stand to:** i.e., defend

153. **lustier:** more vigorous

154. **jacks:** rascals

155. **flirt-gills:** flirting women

156. **skains-mates:** meaning unknown

157. **suffer:** allow

MERCUTIO Yea, is the worst well? Very well took, i'
faith, wisely, wisely.
NURSE If you be he, sir, I desire some confidence with
you.   130
BENVOLIO She will indite him to some supper.
MERCUTIO A bawd, a bawd, a bawd. So ho!
ROMEO What hast thou found?
MERCUTIO No hare, sir, unless a hare, sir, in a Lenten
pie, that is something stale and hoar ere it be spent. 135
⌐Singing.¬   *An old hare hoar,*
               And an old hare hoar,
                 Is very good meat in Lent.
               But a hare that is hoar
               Is too much for a score   140
                 When it hoars ere it be spent.
Romeo, will you come to your father's? We'll to
dinner thither.
ROMEO I will follow you.
MERCUTIO Farewell, ancient lady. Farewell, lady, lady, 145
lady.   ⌐*Mercutio and Benvolio*¬ *exit.*
NURSE I pray you, sir, what saucy merchant was this
that was so full of his ropery?
ROMEO A gentleman, Nurse, that loves to hear himself
talk and will speak more in a minute than he will 150
stand to in a month.
NURSE An he speak anything against me, I'll take him
down, an he were lustier than he is, and twenty
such jacks. An if I cannot, I'll find those that shall.
Scurvy knave, I am none of his flirt-gills; I am none 155
of his skains-mates. ⌐*To Peter.*¬ And thou must stand
by too and suffer every knave to use me at his
pleasure.
PETER I saw no man use you at his pleasure. If I had,
my weapon should quickly have been out. I war- 160
rant you, I dare draw as soon as another man, if I
see occasion in a good quarrel, and the law on my
side.

167. **inquire you out:** find you
169. **in:** i.e., into
174. **weak:** despicable
175. **commend me:** offer my greetings
180. **mark me:** listen to me
184. **shrift:** confession
192. **tackled stair:** rope ladder
193. **topgallant:** summit (literally, the platform atop a mast on a ship)
194. **convoy:** means of conveyance
195. **quit:** reward

NURSE Now, afore God, I am so vexed that every part
about me quivers. Scurvy knave! ⌜*To Romeo.*⌝ Pray   165
you, sir, a word. And, as I told you, my young lady
bid me inquire you out. What she bid me say, I will
keep to myself. But first let me tell you, if you
should lead her in a fool's paradise, as they say, it
were a very gross kind of behavior, as they say. For   170
the gentlewoman is young; and therefore, if you
should deal double with her, truly it were an ill
thing to be offered to any gentlewoman, and very
weak dealing.

ROMEO Nurse, commend me to thy lady and mistress.   175
I protest unto thee—

NURSE Good heart, and i' faith I will tell her as much.
Lord, Lord, she will be a joyful woman.

ROMEO What wilt thou tell her, Nurse? Thou dost not
mark me.   180

NURSE I will tell her, sir, that you do protest, which, as
I take it, is a gentlemanlike offer.

ROMEO   Bid her devise
Some means to come to shrift this afternoon,
And there she shall at Friar Lawrence' cell   185
Be shrived and married. Here is for thy pains.
                    ⌜*Offering her money.*⌝

NURSE No, truly, sir, not a penny.

ROMEO Go to, I say you shall.

NURSE
This afternoon, sir? Well, she shall be there.

ROMEO
And stay, good Nurse, behind the abbey wall.   190
Within this hour my man shall be with thee
And bring thee cords made like a tackled stair,
Which to the high topgallant of my joy
Must be my convoy in the secret night.
Farewell. Be trusty, and I'll quit thy pains.   195
Farewell. Commend me to thy mistress.

200. **counsel:** i.e., a secret

203. **prating:** chattering

204–5. **would . . . aboard:** i.e., is eager to claim her

205. **had as lief:** i.e., would just as happily

209. **clout:** rag; **versal:** i.e., universal

210. **a letter:** i.e., the same letter

212. **that's . . . dog's name:** because the letter *R* may be sounded as a growl

214. **sententious:** the Nurse's mistake for "sentence," i.e., clever saying; **of it:** about it

219. **apace:** quickly

2.5 Juliet waits impatiently for the Nurse to return. Her impatience grows when the Nurse returns but is slow to deliver Romeo's message. Finally Juliet learns that if she wants to marry Romeo, she need only go to Friar Lawrence's cell that afternoon.

———

NURSE
  Now, God in heaven bless thee! Hark you, sir.
ROMEO   What sayst thou, my dear Nurse?
NURSE
  Is your man secret? Did you ne'er hear say
  "Two may keep counsel, putting one away"?   200
ROMEO
  Warrant thee, my man's as true as steel.
NURSE   Well, sir, my mistress is the sweetest lady. Lord,
  Lord, when 'twas a little prating thing—O, there is
  a nobleman in town, one Paris, that would fain lay
  knife aboard, but she, good soul, had as lief see a   205
  toad, a very toad, as see him. I anger her sometimes
  and tell her that Paris is the properer man, but I'll
  warrant you, when I say so, she looks as pale as any
  clout in the versal world. Doth not rosemary and
  Romeo begin both with a letter?   210
ROMEO   Ay, Nurse, what of that? Both with an *R*.
NURSE   Ah, mocker, that's the ⌜dog's⌝ name. *R* is for
  the—No, I know it begins with some other letter,
  and she hath the prettiest sententious of it, of you
  and rosemary, that it would do you good to hear it.   215
ROMEO   Commend me to thy lady.
NURSE   Ay, a thousand times.—Peter.
PETER   Anon.
NURSE   Before and apace.
                                   ⌜*They*⌝ *exit.*

                      ⌜Scene 5⌝
                    Enter Juliet.

JULIET
  The clock struck nine when I did send the Nurse.
  In half an hour she promised to return.
  Perchance she cannot meet him. That's not so.
  O, she is lame! Love's heralds should be thoughts,
  Which ten times faster glides than the sun's beams,   5

6. **louring:** darkly threatening

7. **Therefore . . . Love:** i.e., this is why Love (i.e., Venus, goddess of love) is often represented in a chariot drawn by quick-winged doves

12. **affections:** feelings, emotions

16. **feign as:** act as if

23. **them:** i.e., news (often used in the plural)

26. **Give me leave:** i.e., leave me alone

27. **jaunt:** tiring journey

31. **stay:** wait

35. **in:** i.e., with respect to

Venus and Cupid. (2.5.7–8)
From Joannes ab Indagine, *The book of palmestry* (1666).

104

Driving back shadows over louring hills.
Therefore do nimble-pinioned doves draw Love,
And therefore hath the wind-swift Cupid wings.
Now is the sun upon the highmost hill
Of this day's journey, and from nine till twelve   10
Is ⌜three⌝ long hours, yet she is not come.
Had she affections and warm youthful blood,
She would be as swift in motion as a ball;
My words would bandy her to my sweet love,
And his to me.   15
But old folks, many feign as they were dead,
Unwieldy, slow, heavy, and pale as lead.

Enter Nurse ⌜and Peter.⌝

O God, she comes!—O, honey Nurse, what news?
Hast thou met with him? Send thy man away.
NURSE   Peter, stay at the gate.   ⌜*Peter exits.*⌝ 20
JULIET
  Now, good sweet Nurse—O Lord, why lookest thou
    sad?
  Though news be sad, yet tell them merrily.
  If good, thou shamest the music of sweet news
  By playing it to me with so sour a face.   25
NURSE
  I am aweary. Give me leave awhile.
  Fie, how my bones ache! What a jaunt have I!
JULIET
  I would thou hadst my bones, and I thy news.
  Nay, come, I pray thee, speak. Good, good Nurse,
    speak.   30
NURSE
  Jesu, what haste! Can you not stay awhile?
  Do you not see that I am out of breath?
JULIET
  How art thou out of breath, when thou hast breath
  To say to me that thou art out of breath?
  The excuse that thou dost make in this delay   35

38. **stay the circumstance:** wait for the details
40. **simple:** foolish
44. **on:** about
45. **flower:** best example
53. **o' t' other:** on the other
54. **Beshrew:** curse (here, much milder)
59. **honest:** honorable
66. **God's lady:** the Virgin Mary
67. **hot:** impatient; **Marry, come up, I trow:** an expression of irritation

Is longer than the tale thou dost excuse.
Is thy news good or bad? Answer to that.
Say either, and I'll stay the circumstance.
Let me be satisfied; is 't good or bad?

NURSE Well, you have made a simple choice. You know   40
    not how to choose a man. Romeo? No, not he.
    Though his face be better than any man's, yet his leg
    excels all men's, and for a hand and a foot and a
    body, though they be not to be talked on, yet they
    are past compare. He is not the flower of courtesy,   45
    but I'll warrant him as gentle as a lamb. Go thy
    ways, wench. Serve God. What, have you dined at
    home?

JULIET
No, no. But all this did I know before.
What says he of our marriage? What of that?   50

NURSE
Lord, how my head aches! What a head have I!
It beats as it would fall in twenty pieces.
My back o' t' other side! Ah, my back, my back!
Beshrew your heart for sending me about
To catch my death with jaunting up and down.   55

JULIET
I' faith, I am sorry that thou art not well.
Sweet, sweet, sweet Nurse, tell me, what says my
    love?

NURSE Your love says, like an honest gentleman, and a
    courteous, and a kind, and a handsome, and, I   60
    warrant, a virtuous—Where is your mother?

JULIET
Where is my mother? Why, she is within.
Where should she be? How oddly thou repliest:
"Your love says, like an honest gentleman,
Where is your mother?"   65

NURSE   O God's lady dear,
Are you so hot? Marry, come up, I trow.

70. **coil:** fuss
73. **hie you:** hurry
75. **wanton:** uncontrollable, rebellious
76. **They'll . . . straight:** they turn red immediately
79. **climb a bird's nest:** i.e., climb up to your bedroom
81. **bear the burden:** (1) do your own work; (2) bear the weight of your lover; **soon at night:** i.e., tonight

2.6 Juliet meets Romeo at Friar Lawrence's cell. After expressing their mutual love, they exit with the Friar to be married.

---

3. **But . . . can:** i.e., no matter what sorrow comes
4. **countervail:** i.e., outweigh
6. **Do thou but close:** if you will only join

Is this the poultice for my aching bones?
Henceforward do your messages yourself.

JULIET
Here's such a coil. Come, what says Romeo?   70

NURSE
Have you got leave to go to shrift today?

JULIET   I have.

NURSE
Then hie you hence to Friar Lawrence' cell.
There stays a husband to make you a wife.
Now comes the wanton blood up in your cheeks;   75
They'll be in scarlet straight at any news.
Hie you to church. I must another way,
To fetch a ladder by the which your love
Must climb a bird's nest soon when it is dark.
I am the drudge and toil in your delight,   80
But you shall bear the burden soon at night.
Go. I'll to dinner. Hie you to the cell.

JULIET
Hie to high fortune! Honest Nurse, farewell.
                              They exit.

⌜Scene 6⌝
Enter Friar ⌜Lawrence⌝ and Romeo.

FRIAR LAWRENCE
So smile the heavens upon this holy act
That after-hours with sorrow chide us not.

ROMEO
Amen, amen. But come what sorrow can,
It cannot countervail the exchange of joy
That one short minute gives me in her sight.   5
Do thou but close our hands with holy words,
Then love-devouring death do what he dare,
It is enough I may but call her mine.

FRIAR LAWRENCE
These violent delights have violent ends

10. **powder:** gunpowder
12. **his:** its
13. **confounds:** destroys
15. **Too swift:** i.e., that which goes too fast
18. **gossamers:** cobwebs
19. **idles:** move idly; **wanton:** playful
20. **light:** insubstantial
21. **confessor:** accented on the first and third syllables
24. **measure:** quantity
25. **that:** i.e., if; **more:** greater
26. **blazon:** describe; proclaim
28. **Unfold:** reveal
29. **in either:** in each other; **by:** by means of
30. **Conceit:** understanding
31. **Brags . . . his:** boasts of its
32. **but:** only; **count:** enumerate
34. **sum up sum:** calculate the total
36. **by your leaves:** i.e., begging your pardon
37. **Till . . . one:** i.e., until I, on behalf of the church, make you a married couple

And in their triumph die, like fire and powder,   10
Which, as they kiss, consume. The sweetest honey
Is loathsome in his own deliciousness
And in the taste confounds the appetite.
Therefore love moderately. Long love doth so.
Too swift arrives as tardy as too slow.   15

Enter Juliet.

Here comes the lady. O, so light a foot
Will ne'er wear out the everlasting flint.
A lover may bestride the gossamers
That idles in the wanton summer air,
And yet not fall, so light is vanity.   20

JULIET
Good even to my ghostly confessor.

FRIAR LAWRENCE
Romeo shall thank thee, daughter, for us both.

JULIET
As much to him, else is his thanks too much.

ROMEO
Ah, Juliet, if the measure of thy joy
Be heaped like mine, and that thy skill be more   25
To blazon it, then sweeten with thy breath
This neighbor air, and let rich ⌜music's⌝ tongue
Unfold the imagined happiness that both
Receive in either by this dear encounter.

JULIET
Conceit, more rich in matter than in words,   30
Brags of his substance, not of ornament.
They are but beggars that can count their worth,
But my true love is grown to such excess
I cannot sum up sum of half my wealth.

FRIAR LAWRENCE
Come, come with me, and we will make short work,   35
For, by your leaves, you shall not stay alone
Till Holy Church incorporate two in one.
                                        ⌜*They exit.*⌝

The Tragedy of

ROMEO
AND
JULIET

ACT 3

3.1   Mercutio and Benvolio encounter Tybalt on the street. As soon as Romeo arrives, Tybalt tries to provoke him to fight. When Romeo refuses, Mercutio answers Tybalt's challenge. They duel and Mercutio is fatally wounded. Romeo then avenges Mercutio's death by killing Tybalt in a duel. Benvolio tries to persuade the Prince to excuse Romeo's slaying of Tybalt; however, the Capulets demand that Romeo pay with his life; the Prince instead banishes Romeo from Verona.

---

   2. **Capels:** Capulets
   6. **claps me:** i.e., claps (just as **draws him** [line 9] is Mercutio's way of saying "draws his sword")
   8–9. **by . . . cup:** i.e., by the time his second drink has had an effect on him
   9. **drawer:** waiter
   13–14. **as soon moved . . . moved:** i.e., as soon provoked to be angry and as irritable
   16. **an:** if; **two:** Mercutio deliberately misconstrues Benvolio's "to" as "two."

⌜ACT 3⌝

⌜Scene 1⌝
Enter Mercutio, Benvolio, and ⌜their⌝ men.

BENVOLIO
  I pray thee, good Mercutio, let's retire.
  The day is hot, the Capels ⌜are⌝ abroad,
  And if we meet we shall not 'scape a brawl,
  For now, these hot days, is the mad blood stirring.

MERCUTIO Thou art like one of these fellows that, when   5
  he enters the confines of a tavern, claps me his
  sword upon the table and says "God send me no
  need of thee" and, by the operation of the second
  cup, draws him on the drawer when indeed there is
  no need.   10

BENVOLIO Am I like such a fellow?

MERCUTIO Come, come, thou art as hot a jack in thy
  mood as any in Italy, and as soon moved to be
  moody, and as soon moody to be moved.

BENVOLIO And what to?   15

MERCUTIO Nay, an there were two such, we should
  have none shortly, for one would kill the other.
  Thou—why, thou wilt quarrel with a man that
  hath a hair more or a hair less in his beard than
  thou hast. Thou wilt quarrel with a man for crack-   20
  ing nuts, having no other reason but because thou
  hast hazel eyes. What eye but such an eye would spy
  out such a quarrel? Thy head is as full of quarrels as

24. **meat:** food

24–25. **hath . . . quarreling:** has been beaten into the state of a rotten egg (i.e., has been made addle-headed) as a consequence of your quarreling

29. **doublet:** close-fitting jacket

31. **tutor me from:** teach me to avoid

33. **fee simple:** title to full ownership

35. **simple:** foolish

46. **consortest:** associate

47. **Consort:** play music with (A **consort** is a company of musicians. Mercutio links musicians to minstrels, who were classed with vagabonds.)

49. **fiddlestick:** probably his rapier

50. **Zounds:** i.e., by Christ's wounds, a strong oath

51. **haunt:** meeting place

an egg is full of meat, and yet thy head hath been
beaten as addle as an egg for quarreling. Thou hast   25
quarreled with a man for coughing in the street
because he hath wakened thy dog that hath lain
asleep in the sun. Didst thou not fall out with a tailor
for wearing his new doublet before Easter? With
another, for tying his new shoes with old ribbon?   30
And yet thou wilt tutor me from quarreling?

BENVOLIO   An I were so apt to quarrel as thou art, any
man should buy the fee simple of my life for an
hour and a quarter.

MERCUTIO   The fee simple? O simple!   35

Enter Tybalt, Petruchio, and others.

BENVOLIO   By my head, here comes the Capulets.

MERCUTIO   By my heel, I care not.

TYBALT, ⌜*to his companions*⌝
Follow me close, for I will speak to them.—
Gentlemen, good e'en. A word with one of you.

MERCUTIO   And but one word with one of us? Couple it   40
with something. Make it a word and a blow.

TYBALT   You shall find me apt enough to that, sir, an
you will give me occasion.

MERCUTIO   Could you not take some occasion without
giving?   45

TYBALT   Mercutio, thou consortest with Romeo.

MERCUTIO   Consort? What, dost thou make us minstrels? An thou make minstrels of us, look to hear
nothing but discords. Here's my fiddlestick; here's
that shall make you dance. Zounds, consort!   50

BENVOLIO
We talk here in the public haunt of men.
Either withdraw unto some private place,
Or reason coldly of your grievances,
Or else depart. Here all eyes gaze on us.

58. **your livery:** the uniform of your servants
59. **field:** i.e., place for a duel
64–65. **appertaining rage / To:** rage appropriate in response to
70. **devise:** think out, imagine
71. **of:** i.e., for
72. **tender:** regard
75. **Alla stoccato:** literally, "at the thrust," presumably Mercutio's derisive nickname for Tybalt, the fencing expert; **carries it away:** i.e., wins (because Romeo refuses to fight)
76. **ratcatcher:** "prince of cats"
79. **withal:** with
80. **use:** treat; **dry-beat:** thrash

MERCUTIO
 Men's eyes were made to look, and let them gaze. 55
 I will not budge for no man's pleasure, I.

     Enter Romeo.

TYBALT
 Well, peace be with you, sir. Here comes my man.
MERCUTIO
 But I'll be hanged, sir, if he wear your livery.
 Marry, go before to field, he'll be your follower.
 Your Worship in that sense may call him "man." 60
TYBALT
 Romeo, the love I bear thee can afford
 No better term than this: thou art a villain.
ROMEO
 Tybalt, the reason that I have to love thee
 Doth much excuse the appertaining rage
 To such a greeting. Villain am I none. 65
 Therefore farewell. I see thou knowest me not.
TYBALT
 Boy, this shall not excuse the injuries
 That thou hast done me. Therefore turn and draw.
ROMEO
 I do protest I never injured thee
 But love thee better than thou canst devise 70
 Till thou shalt know the reason of my love.
 And so, good Capulet, which name I tender
 As dearly as mine own, be satisfied.
MERCUTIO
 O calm, dishonorable, vile submission!
 Alla stoccato carries it away. ⌜*He draws.*⌝ 75
 Tybalt, you ratcatcher, will you walk?
TYBALT What wouldst thou have with me?
MERCUTIO Good king of cats, nothing but one of your
  nine lives, that I mean to make bold withal, and, as
  you shall use me hereafter, dry-beat the rest of the 80

81. **pilcher:** A "pilch" is, literally, a leather garment; here, a scabbard.

86. **passado:** a fencing step forward with a thrust

90. **bandying:** fighting

94. **sped:** done for, destroyed

95. **hath nothing:** i.e., has suffered no wound

98. **villain:** i.e., villein, servant

103. **peppered:** finished off, destroyed

106. **book of arithmetic:** i.e., the fencing manual

A street fight. (3.1.86 SD)
From Andreas Friedrich, *Emblemes nouueaux* (1617).

eight. Will you pluck your sword out of his pilcher
by the ears? Make haste, lest mine be about your
ears ere it be out.

TYBALT   I am for you.   ⌈*He draws.*⌉

ROMEO
Gentle Mercutio, put thy rapier up.   85

MERCUTIO   Come, sir, your *passado.*   ⌈*They fight.*⌉

ROMEO
Draw, Benvolio, beat down their weapons.
                                        ⌈*Romeo draws.*⌉
Gentlemen, for shame forbear this outrage!
Tybalt! Mercutio! The Prince expressly hath
Forbid this bandying in Verona streets.   90
Hold, Tybalt! Good Mercutio!
         ⌈*Romeo attempts to beat down their rapiers.*
                        Tybalt stabs Mercutio.⌉

⌈PETRUCHIO⌉   Away, Tybalt!
              ⌈*Tybalt, Petruchio, and their followers exit.*⌉

MERCUTIO   I am hurt.
A plague o' both houses! I am sped.
Is he gone and hath nothing?   95

BENVOLIO   What, art thou hurt?

MERCUTIO
Ay, ay, a scratch, a scratch. Marry, 'tis enough.
Where is my page?—Go, villain, fetch a surgeon.
                                        ⌈*Page exits.*⌉

ROMEO
Courage, man, the hurt cannot be much.

MERCUTIO   No, 'tis not so deep as a well, nor so wide as   100
a church door, but 'tis enough. 'Twill serve. Ask for
me tomorrow, and you shall find me a grave man. I
am peppered, I warrant, for this world. A plague o'
both your houses! Zounds, a dog, a rat, a mouse, a
cat, to scratch a man to death! A braggart, a rogue, a   105
villain that fights by the book of arithmetic! Why the
devil came you between us? I was hurt under your
arm.

112. **worms' meat:** food for worms
114. **near ally:** close relative
115. **very:** true, sincere
118. **cousin:** i.e., kinsman by marriage
120. **in my temper softened valor's steel:** i.e., has made my disposition soft **temper:** temperament (with a glancing reference to the hardening or tempering of steel)
121. **brave:** splendid
122. **aspired:** risen up to
123. **untimely:** prematurely
124. **on more . . . depend:** waits in suspense on the future
125. **others:** future days
128. **respective lenity:** considerate mercifulness
129. **conduct:** guide
131. **late:** recently

ROMEO   I thought all for the best.

MERCUTIO
Help me into some house, Benvolio,   110
Or I shall faint. A plague o' both your houses!
They have made worms' meat of me.
I have it, and soundly, too. Your houses!
                 ⌜*All but Romeo*⌝ *exit.*

ROMEO
This gentleman, the Prince's near ally,
My very friend, hath got this mortal hurt   115
In my behalf. My reputation stained
With Tybalt's slander—Tybalt, that an hour
Hath been my cousin! O sweet Juliet,
Thy beauty hath made me effeminate
And in my temper softened valor's steel.   120

Enter Benvolio.

BENVOLIO
O Romeo, Romeo, brave Mercutio is dead.
That gallant spirit hath aspired the clouds,
Which too untimely here did scorn the earth.

ROMEO
This day's black fate on more days doth depend.
This but begins the woe others must end.   125

⌜*Enter Tybalt.*⌝

BENVOLIO
Here comes the furious Tybalt back again.

ROMEO
⌜Alive⌝ in triumph, and Mercutio slain!
Away to heaven, respective lenity,
And ⌜fire-eyed⌝ fury be my conduct now.—
Now, Tybalt, take the "villain" back again   130
That late thou gavest me, for Mercutio's soul
Is but a little way above our heads,
Staying for thine to keep him company.
Either thou or I, or both, must go with him.

139. **up:** i.e., up in arms

140. **amazed:** astounded; **doom thee death:** condemn you to death

142. **fool:** plaything

150. **discover:** reveal

151. **manage:** course

VINCENTIO

S A V I O L O

his Practiſe.

Jn two Bookes.

The firſt intreating of the vſe of the Rapier and Dagger.

The ſecond, of Honor and honorable Quarrels.

LONDON

Printed by IOHN WOLFE.

1 5 9 5.

A fencing manual. (3.1.106)
From Vincentio Saviolo, *His practise* (1594).

TYBALT
  Thou, wretched boy, that didst consort him here,   135
  Shalt with him hence.
ROMEO   This shall determine that.
                              They fight. Tybalt falls.

BENVOLIO
  Romeo, away, begone!
  The citizens are up, and Tybalt slain.
  Stand not amazed. The Prince will doom thee death   140
  If thou art taken. Hence, be gone, away.
ROMEO
  O, I am Fortune's fool!
BENVOLIO   Why dost thou stay?
                              Romeo exits.

              Enter Citizens.

CITIZEN
  Which way ran he that killed Mercutio?
  Tybalt, that murderer, which way ran he?   145
BENVOLIO
  There lies that Tybalt.
CITIZEN, ⌜*to Tybalt*⌝   Up, sir, go with me.
  I charge thee in the Prince's name, obey.

Enter Prince, old Montague, Capulet, their Wives and all.

PRINCE
  Where are the vile beginners of this fray?
BENVOLIO
  O noble Prince, I can discover all   150
  The unlucky manage of this fatal brawl.
  There lies the man, slain by young Romeo,
  That slew thy kinsman, brave Mercutio.
LADY CAPULET
  Tybalt, my cousin, O my brother's child!
  O Prince! O cousin! Husband! O, the blood is spilled 155
  Of my dear kinsman! Prince, as thou art true,

161. **fair:** politely; **bethink:** reflect upon
162. **nice:** trivial, trifling; **withal:** in addition
165. **take truce with:** placate; **spleen:** i.e., anger
166. **tilts:** strikes
172. **Retorts it:** sends it back again
177. **envious:** malicious
178. **stout:** valiant
180. **entertained:** contemplated
186. **Affection:** i.e., inclination toward them

For blood of ours, shed blood of Montague.
O cousin, cousin!

PRINCE
Benvolio, who began this bloody fray?

BENVOLIO
Tybalt, here slain, whom Romeo's hand did slay.   160
Romeo, that spoke him fair, bid him bethink
How nice the quarrel was, and urged withal
Your high displeasure. All this utterèd
With gentle breath, calm look, knees humbly bowed
Could not take truce with the unruly spleen   165
Of Tybalt, deaf to peace, but that he tilts
With piercing steel at bold Mercutio's breast,
Who, all as hot, turns deadly point to point
And, with a martial scorn, with one hand beats
Cold death aside and with the other sends   170
It back to Tybalt, whose dexterity
Retorts it. Romeo he cries aloud
"Hold, friends! Friends, part!" and swifter than his
    tongue
His ⌜agile⌝ arm beats down their fatal points,   175
And 'twixt them rushes; underneath whose arm
An envious thrust from Tybalt hit the life
Of stout Mercutio, and then Tybalt fled.
But by and by comes back to Romeo,
Who had but newly entertained revenge,   180
And to 't they go like lightning, for, ere I
Could draw to part them, was stout Tybalt slain,
And, as he fell, did Romeo turn and fly.
This is the truth, or let Benvolio die.

LADY CAPULET
He is a kinsman to the Montague.   185
Affection makes him false; he speaks not true.
Some twenty of them fought in this black strife,
And all those twenty could but kill one life.
I beg for justice, which thou, Prince, must give.
Romeo slew Tybalt; Romeo must not live.   190

192. **his dear blood:** i.e., Mercutio's blood

194. **concludes but:** only concludes; **should end:** should have ended

198. **I:** The Prince switches from the royal "we" of line 197 to express a personal, rather than merely official, interest in the feud.

199. **My blood:** i.e., my kinsman (Mercutio)

200. **amerce:** punish

203. **Nor tears:** i.e., neither tears; **purchase out:** i.e., buy impunity for

206. **attend:** pay attention to, heed

3.2 Juliet longs for Romeo to come to her. The Nurse arrives with the news that Romeo has killed Tybalt and has been banished. Juliet at first feels grief for the loss of her cousin Tybalt and verbally attacks Romeo, but then renounces these feelings and devotes herself to grief for Romeo's banishment. The Nurse promises to bring Romeo to Juliet that night.

———

1–2. **Gallop . . . lodging:** addressed to the horses of Phoebus, the sun god, urging speed

2. **wagoner:** charioteer

3. **Phaeton:** the son of Phoebus, allowed to drive the chariot of the sun but unable to control the horses.

5. **close curtain:** i.e., curtain of secrecy

6. **runaways:** perhaps, vagabonds; **wink:** i.e., shut, close

9. **By:** i.e., by the light of

PRINCE
　Romeo slew him; he slew Mercutio.
　Who now the price of his dear blood doth owe?
⌜MONTAGUE⌝
　Not Romeo, Prince; he was Mercutio's friend.
　His fault concludes but what the law should end,
　The life of Tybalt.   195
PRINCE　　　　　　And for that offense
　Immediately we do exile him hence.
　I have an interest in your hearts' proceeding:
　My blood for your rude brawls doth lie a-bleeding.
　But I'll amerce you with so strong a fine   200
　That you shall all repent the loss of mine.
　⌜I⌝ will be deaf to pleading and excuses.
　Nor tears nor prayers shall purchase out abuses.
　Therefore use none. Let Romeo hence in haste,
　Else, when he is found, that hour is his last.   205
　Bear hence this body and attend our will.
　Mercy but murders, pardoning those that kill.
　　　　　　　　　　⌜*They*⌝ *exit,* ⌜*the Capulet men*
　　　　　　　　　　　　bearing off Tybalt's body.⌝

⌜Scene 2⌝
Enter Juliet alone.

JULIET
　Gallop apace, you fiery-footed steeds,
　Towards Phoebus' lodging. Such a wagoner
　As Phaeton would whip you to the west
　And bring in cloudy night immediately.
　Spread thy close curtain, love-performing night,   5
　That runaways' eyes may wink, and Romeo
　Leap to these arms, untalked of and unseen.
　Lovers can see to do their amorous rites
　By their own beauties, or, if love be blind,

10. **civil:** i.e., soberly dressed

12. **learn:** teach

14–15. **Hood . . . mantle:** i.e., cover my blushes with your dark cloak (The language is from falconry. An untamed [**unmanned**] falcon beat its wings [**bating**] unless its head was covered with a black **hood**.)

15. **strange:** unfamiliar

16. **Think:** i.e., and think

23. **I:** often changed by editors to "he"

28. **mansion:** dwelling place

33 SD. **cords:** i.e., the rope ladder

A hooded falcon. (3.2.14)
From Antonio Francesco Doni, *L'academia Peregrina* (1552).

It best agrees with night. Come, civil night,   10
Thou sober-suited matron all in black,
And learn me how to lose a winning match
Played for a pair of stainless maidenhoods.
Hood my unmanned blood, bating in my cheeks,
With thy black mantle till strange love grow bold,   15
Think true love acted simple modesty.
Come, night. Come, Romeo. Come, thou day in
    night,
For thou wilt lie upon the wings of night
Whiter than new snow upon a raven's back.   20
Come, gentle night; come, loving black-browed
    night,
Give me my Romeo, and when I shall die,
Take him and cut him out in little stars,
And he will make the face of heaven so fine   25
That all the world will be in love with night
And pay no worship to the garish sun.
O, I have bought the mansion of a love
But not possessed it, and, though I am sold,
Not yet enjoyed. So tedious is this day   30
As is the night before some festival
To an impatient child that hath new robes
And may not wear them.

                  Enter Nurse with cords.

                        O, here comes my nurse,
And she brings news, and every tongue that speaks   35
But Romeo's name speaks heavenly eloquence.—
Now, Nurse, what news? What hast thou there? The
    cords
That Romeo bid thee fetch?
NURSE   Ay, ay, the cords.   40
                        ⌜*Dropping the rope ladder.*⌝
JULIET
Ay me, what news? Why dost thou wring thy hands?

42. **weraday:** welladay, an expression of sorrow

45. **envious:** malicious

52. **"I":** pronounced the same as **ay,** which means "yes"

53. **cockatrice:** a mythical serpent (with the head, wings, and feet of a cock) whose look could kill

55. **those eyes:** i.e., Romeo's eyes

57. **weal:** well-being, happiness

59. **God save the mark:** a superstitious expression

60. **corse:** i.e., corpse

62. **gore:** clotted

63. **bankrout:** i.e., bankrupt

65. **Vile . . . resign:** i.e., let my body (itself, according to the Bible, originally made from dust or **vile earth**) be committed to the earth

66. **press . . . bier:** i.e., weigh down a single bier

A cockatrice. (3.2.53)
From Joachim Camerarius, *Symbolorum et emblematum* (1605).

NURSE
　Ah weraday, he's dead, he's dead, he's dead!
　We are undone, lady, we are undone.
　Alack the day, he's gone, he's killed, he's dead.
JULIET
　Can heaven be so envious?   45
NURSE   Romeo can,
　Though heaven cannot. O Romeo, Romeo,
　Whoever would have thought it? Romeo!
JULIET
　˅ What devil art thou that dost torment me thus?
　This torture should be roared in dismal hell. ˗   50
　Hath Romeo slain himself? Say thou but "Ay,"
　And that bare vowel "I" shall poison more
　Than the death-darting eye of cockatrice.
　I am not I if there be such an "I,"
　Or those eyes ⌈shut⌉ that makes thee answer "Ay."   55
　If he be slain, say "Ay," or if not, "No."
　Brief sounds determine my weal or woe.
NURSE
　I saw the wound. I saw it with mine eyes
　(God save the mark!) here on his manly breast—
　A piteous corse, a bloody piteous corse,   60
　Pale, pale as ashes, all bedaubed in blood,
　All in gore blood. I swoonèd at the sight.
JULIET
　O break, my heart, poor bankrout, break at once!
　To prison, eyes; ne'er look on liberty.
　Vile earth to earth resign; end motion here,   65
　And thou and Romeo press one heavy bier.
NURSE
　O Tybalt, Tybalt, the best friend I had!
　O courteous Tybalt, honest gentleman,
　That ever I should live to see thee dead!
JULIET
　What storm is this that blows so contrary?   70

73. **dreadful ... doom:** i.e., let the trumpet be blown to announce the Last Judgment

79. **hid with:** hidden by

80. **keep:** dwell in

82. **wolvish-ravening:** i.e., wolfishly devouring

83. **show:** appearance

84. **Just:** exact; **justly:** truly

87. **bower:** i.e., give a dwelling to

94. **naught:** evil; **dissemblers:** deceivers

95. **aqua vitae:** strong drink, usually brandy

Is Romeo slaughtered and is Tybalt dead?
My dearest cousin, and my dearer lord?
Then, dreadful trumpet, sound the general doom,
For who is living if those two are gone?
NURSE
    Tybalt is gone and Romeo banishèd.   75
    Romeo that killed him—he is banishèd.
JULIET
    O God, did Romeo's hand shed Tybalt's blood?
⌜NURSE⌝
    It did, it did, alas the day, it did.
⌜JULIET⌝
    O serpent heart hid with a flow'ring face!
    Did ever dragon keep so fair a cave?   80
    Beautiful tyrant, fiend angelical!
    Dove-feathered raven, wolvish-ravening lamb!
    Despisèd substance of divinest show!
    Just opposite to what thou justly seem'st,
    A ⌜damnèd⌝ saint, an honorable villain.   85
    O nature, what hadst thou to do in hell
    When thou didst bower the spirit of a fiend
    In mortal paradise of such sweet flesh?
    Was ever book containing such vile matter
    So fairly bound? O, that deceit should dwell   90
    In such a gorgeous palace!
NURSE   There's no trust,
    No faith, no honesty in men. All perjured,
    All forsworn, all naught, all dissemblers.
    Ah, where's my man? Give me some aqua vitae.   95
    These griefs, these woes, these sorrows make me
        old.
    Shame come to Romeo!
JULIET   Blistered be thy tongue
    For such a wish! He was not born to shame.   100
    Upon his brow shame is ashamed to sit,
    For 'tis a throne where honor may be crowned

107. **poor my lord:** i.e., my poor lord

110. **wherefore:** why

113. **Your . . . woe:** i.e., tears are properly the tribute (i.e., tax) paid to sorrow

131. **Which . . . moved:** i.e., which might have provoked ordinary mourning   **modern:** everyday

132. **a rearward:** the rearguard of a marching army (Juliet has been comparing the Nurse's speech to an army: see **ranked** [line 128]. In the first rank or vanguard is the statement "Tybalt's dead"; behind it, in the rear, is "Romeo is banishèd.")

136. **bound:** boundary

Sole monarch of the universal earth.
O, what a beast was I to chide at him!

NURSE
Will you speak well of him that killed your cousin?　105

JULIET
Shall I speak ill of him that is my husband?
Ah, poor my lord, what tongue shall smooth thy
　name
When I, thy three-hours wife, have mangled it?
But wherefore, villain, didst thou kill my cousin?　110
That villain cousin would have killed my husband.
Back, foolish tears, back to your native spring;
Your tributary drops belong to woe,
Which you, mistaking, offer up to joy.
My husband lives, that Tybalt would have slain,　115
And Tybalt's dead, that would have slain my
　husband.
All this is comfort. Wherefore weep I then?
Some word there was, worser than Tybalt's death,
That murdered me. I would forget it fain,　120
But, O, it presses to my memory
Like damnèd guilty deeds to sinners' minds:
"Tybalt is dead and Romeo banishèd."
That "banishèd," that one word "banishèd,"
Hath slain ten thousand Tybalts. Tybalt's death　125
Was woe enough if it had ended there;
Or, if sour woe delights in fellowship
And needly will be ranked with other griefs,
Why followed not, when she said "Tybalt's dead,"
"Thy father" or "thy mother," nay, or both,　130
Which modern lamentation might have moved?
But with a rearward following Tybalt's death,
"Romeo is banishèd." To speak that word
Is father, mother, Tybalt, Romeo, Juliet,
All slain, all dead. "Romeo is banishèd."　135
There is no end, no limit, measure, bound,

137. **that word's death:** i.e., the death expressed by the word **banishèd; sound:** (1) express; (2) measure (i.e., by taking soundings to determine its depth)
145. **you are beguiled:** your hopes are cheated
151. **Hie:** hurry
152. **wot:** know

3.3 Friar Lawrence tells Romeo that his punishment for killing Tybalt is banishment, not death. Romeo responds that death is preferable to banishment from Juliet. When the Nurse enters and tells Romeo that Juliet is grief-stricken, Romeo attempts suicide. Friar Lawrence then says that Romeo may spend the night with Juliet and leave for exile in Mantua next morning. The Friar promises that Balthasar will bring Romeo news of Verona and suggests that Romeo can expect in time that the Prince may relent and allow him to return to Verona.

———————

2. **Affliction . . . parts:** i.e., it is as if disaster were in love with your attractive qualities

In that word's death. No words can that woe sound.
Where is my father and my mother, Nurse?

NURSE

Weeping and wailing over Tybalt's corse.
Will you go to them? I will bring you thither.   140

JULIET

Wash they his wounds with tears? Mine shall be
    spent,
When theirs are dry, for Romeo's banishment.—
Take up those cords.
                    ⌜*The Nurse picks up the rope ladder.*⌝
                          Poor ropes, you are beguiled,   145
Both you and I, for Romeo is exiled.
He made you for a highway to my bed,
But I, a maid, die maiden-widowèd.
Come, cords—come, Nurse. I'll to my wedding bed,
And death, not Romeo, take my maidenhead!   150

NURSE

Hie to your chamber. I'll find Romeo
To comfort you. I wot well where he is.
Hark you, your Romeo will be here at night.
I'll to him. He is hid at Lawrence' cell.

JULIET

O, find him!   ⌜*Giving the Nurse a ring.*⌝ 155
              Give this ring to my true knight
And bid him come to take his last farewell.
                              ⌜*They*⌝ *exit.*

              ⌜Scene 3⌝
          Enter Friar ⌜*Lawrence.*⌝

FRIAR LAWRENCE

Romeo, come forth; come forth, thou fearful man.
Affliction is enamored of thy parts,
And thou art wedded to calamity.

4. **doom:** sentence, judgment

5. **craves acquaintance at my hand:** is anxious to meet me (literally, to shake hands with me)

11. **vanished:** disappeared (a reference to words as mere breath that vanish as soon as spoken)

14. **his:** its

17. **patient:** calm

18. **without:** outside

21. **world's exile:** exile from the world

22. **mistermed:** misnamed

26. **Thy fault . . . death:** i.e., your crime is punishable by death under our law

27. **part:** side; **rushed aside:** shoved aside

⌜*Enter Romeo.*⌝

ROMEO
 Father, what news? What is the Prince's doom?
 What sorrow craves acquaintance at my hand   5
 That I yet know not?
FRIAR LAWRENCE   Too familiar
 Is my dear son with such sour company.
 I bring thee tidings of the Prince's doom.
ROMEO
 What less than doomsday is the Prince's doom? 10
FRIAR LAWRENCE
 A gentler judgment vanished from his lips:
 Not body's death, but body's banishment.
ROMEO
 Ha, banishment? Be merciful, say "death,"
 For exile hath more terror in his look,
 Much more than death. Do not say "banishment." 15
FRIAR LAWRENCE
 Here from Verona art thou banishèd.
 Be patient, for the world is broad and wide.
ROMEO
 There is no world without Verona walls
 But purgatory, torture, hell itself.
 Hence "banishèd" is "banished from the world," 20
 And world's exile is death. Then "banishèd"
 Is death mistermed. Calling death "banishèd,"
 Thou cutt'st my head off with a golden ax
 And smilest upon the stroke that murders me.
FRIAR LAWRENCE
 O deadly sin, O rude unthankfulness! 25
 Thy fault our law calls death, but the kind Prince,
 Taking thy part, hath rushed aside the law
 And turned that black word "death" to
  "banishment."
 This is dear mercy, and thou seest it not. 30

36. **courtship:** status as a courtier
40. **vestal:** i.e., virginal
41. **Still:** always; **their own kisses:** i.e., the kisses each lip gives the other
48. **mean:** means; **mean:** sordid
51. **attends:** accompanies
53. **professed:** self-proclaimed
55. **fond:** foolish
60. **Yet:** still

ROMEO
'Tis torture and not mercy. Heaven is here
Where Juliet lives, and every cat and dog
And little mouse, every unworthy thing,
Live here in heaven and may look on her,
But Romeo may not. More validity,   35
More honorable state, more courtship lives
In carrion flies than Romeo. They may seize
On the white wonder of dear Juliet's hand
And steal immortal blessing from her lips,
Who even in pure and vestal modesty   40
Still blush, as thinking their own kisses sin;
But Romeo may not; he is banishèd.
Flies may do this, but I from this must fly.
They are free men, but I am banishèd.
And sayest thou yet that exile is not death?   45
Hadst thou no poison mixed, no sharp-ground
    knife,
No sudden mean of death, though ne'er so mean,
But "banishèd" to kill me? "Banishèd"?
O Friar, the damnèd use that word in hell.   50
Howling attends it. How hast thou the heart,
Being a divine, a ghostly confessor,
A sin absolver, and my friend professed,
To mangle me with that word "banishèd"?

FRIAR LAWRENCE
⌐Thou⌐ fond mad man, hear me a little speak.   55

ROMEO
O, thou wilt speak again of banishment.

FRIAR LAWRENCE
I'll give thee armor to keep off that word,
Adversity's sweet milk, philosophy,
To comfort thee, though thou art banishèd.

ROMEO
Yet "banishèd"? Hang up philosophy.   60
Unless philosophy can make a Juliet,

62. **Displant:** uproot
65. **when that:** when
66. **dispute:** reason; **of:** about; **estate:** condition
70. **Doting:** in love
81. **By and by:** soon (addressed to the person knocking)
82. **simpleness:** foolishness

Displant a town, reverse a prince's doom,
It helps not, it prevails not. Talk no more.

FRIAR LAWRENCE
O, then I see that ⌜madmen⌝ have no ears.

ROMEO
How should they when that wise men have no eyes? 65

FRIAR LAWRENCE
Let me dispute with thee of thy estate.

ROMEO
Thou canst not speak of that thou dost not feel.
Wert thou as young as I, Juliet thy love,
An hour but married, Tybalt murderèd,
Doting like me, and like me banishèd, 70
Then mightst thou speak, then mightst thou tear thy
hair
And fall upon the ground as I do now,
⌜*Romeo throws himself down.*⌝
Taking the measure of an unmade grave.
Knock ⌜*within.*⌝

FRIAR LAWRENCE
Arise. One knocks. Good Romeo, hide thyself. 75

ROMEO
Not I, unless the breath of heartsick groans,
Mistlike, enfold me from the search of eyes.
Knock.

FRIAR LAWRENCE
Hark, how they knock!—Who's there?—Romeo,
arise.
Thou wilt be taken.—Stay awhile.—Stand up. 80
Knock.
Run to my study.—By and by.—God's will,
What simpleness is this?—I come, I come.
Knock.
Who knocks so hard? Whence come you? What's
your will?

92. **even:** exactly; **case:** plight

93. **woeful sympathy:** i.e., harmony (between Romeo and Juliet) in their grief

106. **My concealed lady:** i.e., she who is secretly my wife (**concealed** accented on the first syllable); **canceled:** annulled (because of his banishment)

109. **on Romeo:** i.e., on the name "Romeo"

NURSE, ⌜*within*⌝
  Let me come in, and you shall know my errand.   85
  I come from Lady Juliet.
FRIAR LAWRENCE, ⌜*admitting the Nurse*⌝
                    Welcome then.

        ⌜*Enter Nurse.*⌝

NURSE
  O holy Friar, O, tell me, holy Friar,
  Where's my lady's lord? Where's Romeo?
FRIAR LAWRENCE
  There on the ground, with his own tears made   90
    drunk.
NURSE
  O, he is even in my mistress' case,
  Just in her case. O woeful sympathy!
  Piteous predicament! Even so lies she,
  Blubb'ring and weeping, weeping and blubb'ring.—   95
  Stand up, stand up. Stand an you be a man.
  For Juliet's sake, for her sake, rise and stand.
  Why should you fall into so deep an O?
ROMEO   Nurse.
NURSE
  Ah sir, ah sir, death's the end of all.   100
ROMEO, ⌜*rising up*⌝
  Spakest thou of Juliet? How is it with her?
  Doth not she think me an old murderer,
  Now I have stained the childhood of our joy
  With blood removed but little from her own?
  Where is she? And how doth she? And what says   105
  My concealed lady to our canceled love?
NURSE
  O, she says nothing, sir, but weeps and weeps,
  And now falls on her bed, and then starts up,
  And "Tybalt" calls, and then on Romeo cries,
  And then down falls again.   110

112. **level:** aim

116. **sack:** destroy by plundering and pillaging

122. **Unseemly:** improper (even for a woman); **seeming:** apparent

123. **ill-beseeming . . . both:** i.e., unnatural animal in appearing to be both a woman and a man

125. **tempered:** adjusted

129. **railest . . . on:** heap scorn upon, revile

132–44. **thou shamest . . . defense:** In these lines the Friar shows, in turn, how Romeo is shaming his form as a man, his love for Juliet, and his intelligence (**wit**). Like a **usurer** (one who, contrary to the morality of the time, lent money to get interest), Romeo has an abundance of wealth (his **shape**, **love**, and **wit**) but does not use any of it properly.

133. **Which:** who

136. **but . . . wax:** no better than a wax figure

137. **Digressing from:** if it swerves away from

138. **dear love sworn:** love you have sworn is dear

139. **Killing:** in that it kills

141. **conduct:** management

142. **powder:** gunpowder; **flask:** powder flask

144. **thou dismembered . . . defense:** i.e., you are blown to pieces by your own weapons

146. **thou . . . dead:** i.e., you were just now willing to die

ROMEO As if that name,
    Shot from the deadly level of a gun,
    Did murder her, as that name's cursèd hand
    Murdered her kinsman.—O, tell me, Friar, tell me,
    In what vile part of this anatomy   115
    Doth my name lodge? Tell me, that I may sack
    The hateful mansion.   ⌜*He draws his dagger.*⌝
FRIAR LAWRENCE   Hold thy desperate hand!
    Art thou a man? Thy form cries out thou art.
    Thy tears are womanish; thy wild acts ⌜denote⌝   120
    The unreasonable fury of a beast.
    Unseemly woman in a seeming man,
    And ill-beseeming beast in seeming both!
    Thou hast amazed me. By my holy order,
    I thought thy disposition better tempered.   125
    Hast thou slain Tybalt? Wilt thou slay thyself,
    And slay thy lady that in thy life ⌜lives,⌝
    By doing damnèd hate upon thyself?
    Why railest thou on thy birth, the heaven, and earth,
    Since birth and heaven and earth, all three do meet 130
    In thee at once, which thou at once wouldst lose?
    Fie, fie, thou shamest thy shape, thy love, thy wit,
    Which, like a usurer, abound'st in all
    And usest none in that true use indeed
    Which should bedeck thy shape, thy love, thy wit.   135
    Thy noble shape is but a form of wax,
    Digressing from the valor of a man;
    Thy dear love sworn but hollow perjury,
    Killing that love which thou hast vowed to cherish;
    Thy wit, that ornament to shape and love,   140
    Misshapen in the conduct of them both,
    Like powder in a skilless soldier's flask,
    Is set afire by thine own ignorance,
    And thou dismembered with thine own defense.
    What, rouse thee, man! Thy Juliet is alive,   145
    For whose dear sake thou wast but lately dead:

147. **happy:** fortunate; **would:** wanted to
150. **exile:** accent on the second syllable
154. **fortune:** i.e., good fortune
155. **such:** i.e., such ungrateful persons
156. **decreed:** decided
158. **look:** i.e., look that, be sure that; **watch:** guards stationed at the city gates
159. **pass:** i.e., leave Verona
161. **blaze:** make public; **friends:** relatives (the warring Capulets and Montagues)
165. **Commend:** i.e., offer my respects
167. **apt unto:** inclined to do

There art thou happy. Tybalt would kill thee,
But thou slewest Tybalt: there art thou happy.
The law that threatened death becomes thy friend
And turns it to exile: there art thou happy.   150
A pack of blessings light upon thy back;
Happiness courts thee in her best array;
But, like a ⌜misbehaved⌝ and sullen wench,
Thou ⌜pouts upon⌝ thy fortune and thy love.
Take heed, take heed, for such die miserable.   155
Go, get thee to thy love, as was decreed.
Ascend her chamber. Hence and comfort her.
But look thou stay not till the watch be set,
For then thou canst not pass to Mantua,
Where thou shalt live till we can find a time   160
To blaze your marriage, reconcile your friends,
Beg pardon of the Prince, and call thee back
With twenty hundred thousand times more joy
Than thou went'st forth in lamentation.—
Go before, Nurse. Commend me to thy lady,   165
And bid her hasten all the house to bed,
Which heavy sorrow makes them apt unto.
Romeo is coming.

NURSE
O Lord, I could have stayed here all the night
To hear good counsel. O, what learning is!—   170
My lord, I'll tell my lady you will come.

ROMEO
Do so, and bid my sweet prepare to chide.

NURSE
Here, sir, a ring she bid me give you, sir.
                    ⌜*Nurse gives Romeo a ring.*⌝
Hie you, make haste, for it grows very late.
                              ⌜*She exits.*⌝

ROMEO
How well my comfort is revived by this!   175

176–77. **here stands all your state:** your condition depends on the following

180. **find out your man:** search out your servant

181–82. **signify . . . to you:** i.e., let you know every piece of good fortune

185. **brief:** quickly

3.4 Paris again approaches Capulet about marrying Juliet. Capulet, saying that Juliet will do as she is told, promises Paris that she will marry him in three days.

---

1. **fallen out:** happened

2. **move our daughter:** i.e., persuade Juliet

6. **but:** except

12. **mewed up to:** shut up with (The term is from falconry and means "caged."); **heaviness:** grief

13. **desperate tender:** bold (or risky) offer

FRIAR LAWRENCE
  Go hence, good night—and here stands all your
    state:
  Either be gone before the watch be set
  Or by the break of day ⌜disguised⌝ from hence.
  Sojourn in Mantua. I'll find out your man,   180
  And he shall signify from time to time
  Every good hap to you that chances here.
  Give me thy hand. 'Tis late. Farewell. Good night.
ROMEO
  But that a joy past joy calls out on me,
  It were a grief so brief to part with thee.   185
  Farewell.

                                                  They exit.

                          ⌜Scene 4⌝
              Enter old Capulet, his Wife, and Paris.

CAPULET
  Things have fallen out, sir, so unluckily
  That we have had no time to move our daughter.
  Look you, she loved her kinsman Tybalt dearly,
  And so did I. Well, we were born to die.
  'Tis very late. She'll not come down tonight.   5
  I promise you, but for your company,
  I would have been abed an hour ago.
PARIS
  These times of woe afford no times to woo.—
  Madam, good night. Commend me to your
    daughter.   10
LADY CAPULET
  I will, and know her mind early tomorrow.
  Tonight she's mewed up to her heaviness.
CAPULET
  Sir Paris, I will make a desperate tender
  Of my child's love. I think she will ⌜be⌝ ruled

17. **son:** future son-in-law
18. **mark you me?:** i.e., do you hear?
26. **We'll . . . ado:** i.e., we won't make much of a fuss
27. **late:** recently
28. **held him carelessly:** i.e., esteemed him little
35. **against:** in preparation for
37. **Afore me:** a mild oath

3.5 Romeo and Juliet separate at the first light of day. Just after Romeo has descended from Juliet's room, her mother comes to announce that Juliet must marry Paris. When Juliet refuses, her father becomes enraged and vows to put her out on the streets if she will not accept Paris as her husband. The Nurse recommends that Juliet forget the banished Romeo and regard Paris as a more desirable husband. Juliet is secretly outraged at the Nurse's advice and decides to seek Friar Lawrence's help.

———————

0 SD. **aloft:** i.e., in the gallery above the stage
3. **fearful:** anxious

In all respects by me. Nay, more, I doubt it not.—   15
Wife, go you to her ere you go to bed.
Acquaint her here of my son Paris' love,
And bid her—mark you me?—on Wednesday
    next—
But soft, what day is this?   20
PARIS   Monday, my lord.
CAPULET
Monday, ha ha! Well, Wednesday is too soon.
O' Thursday let it be.—O' Thursday, tell her,
She shall be married to this noble earl.—
Will you be ready? Do you like this haste?   25
⌜We'll⌝ keep no great ado: a friend or two.
For hark you, Tybalt being slain so late,
It may be thought we held him carelessly,
Being our kinsman, if we revel much.
Therefore we'll have some half a dozen friends,   30
And there an end. But what say you to Thursday?
PARIS
My lord, I would that Thursday were tomorrow.
CAPULET
Well, get you gone. O' Thursday be it, then.
⌜*To Lady Capulet.*⌝ Go you to Juliet ere you go to bed.
Prepare her, wife, against this wedding day.—   35
Farewell, my lord.—Light to my chamber, ho!—
Afore me, it is so very late that we
May call it early by and by.—Good night.
                              They exit.

                    ⌜Scene 5⌝
          Enter Romeo and Juliet aloft.

JULIET
Wilt thou be gone? It is not yet near day.
It was the nightingale, and not the lark,
That pierced the fearful hollow of thine ear.

7. **envious:** malicious

9. **Night's candles:** i.e., the stars

13. **exhaled:** drew up as a gas (A meteor was thought to be a fiery gas drawn up by the sun.)

18. **so thou:** i.e., if thou

19. **the morning's eye:** See 2.3.1, where the morn is "gray-eyed."

20. **reflex of Cynthia's brow:** i.e., the moon's reflection   **Cynthia:** goddess of the moon

23. **care, will:** desire

28. **sharps:** discordant notes (above the true pitch)

29. **division:** a rapid, melodious passage of music

33. **affray:** frighten

34. **hunt's-up:** i.e., an early morning song

Nightly she sings on yond pomegranate tree.
Believe me, love, it was the nightingale.   5
ROMEO
　It was the lark, the herald of the morn,
　No nightingale. Look, love, what envious streaks
　Do lace the severing clouds in yonder east.
　Night's candles are burnt out, and jocund day
　Stands tiptoe on the misty mountain-tops.   10
　I must be gone and live, or stay and die.
JULIET
　Yond light is not daylight, I know it, I.
　It is some meteor that the sun ⌜exhaled⌝
　To be to thee this night a torchbearer
　And light thee on thy way to Mantua.   15
　Therefore stay yet. Thou need'st not to be gone.
ROMEO
　Let me be ta'en; let me be put to death.
　I am content, so thou wilt have it so.
　I'll say yon gray is not the morning's eye;
　'Tis but the pale reflex of Cynthia's brow.   20
　Nor that is not the lark whose notes do beat
　The vaulty heaven so high above our heads.
　I have more care to stay than will to go.
　Come death and welcome. Juliet wills it so.
　How is 't, my soul? Let's talk. It is not day.   25
JULIET
　It is, it is. Hie hence, begone, away!
　It is the lark that sings so out of tune,
　Straining harsh discords and unpleasing sharps.
　Some say the lark makes sweet division.
　This doth not so, for she divideth us.   30
　Some say the lark and loathèd toad ⌜changed⌝ eyes.
　O, now I would they had changed voices too,
　Since arm from arm that voice doth us affray,
　Hunting thee hence with hunt's-up to the day.
　O, now begone. More light and light it grows.   35

46. **by this count:** according to this calculation; **much in years:** i.e., very old

54. **ill-divining:** prophetic of evil

55. **Methinks:** I think

59. **Dry . . . blood:** i.e., we are pale with grief (Sorrow is represented as thirsty because it was believed that each sorrowful sigh consumed a drop of blood from the heart.)

ROMEO
    More light and light, more dark and dark our woes.

                    Enter Nurse.

NURSE   Madam.
JULIET   Nurse?
NURSE
    Your lady mother is coming to your chamber.
    The day is broke; be wary; look about.   ⌜*She exits.*⌝   40
JULIET
    Then, window, let day in, and let life out.
ROMEO
    Farewell, farewell. One kiss and I'll descend.
                    ⌜*They kiss, and Romeo descends.*⌝
JULIET
    Art thou gone so? Love, lord, ay husband, friend!
    I must hear from thee every day in the hour,
    For in a minute there are many days.   45
    O, by this count I shall be much in years
    Ere I again behold my Romeo.
ROMEO   Farewell.
    I will omit no opportunity
    That may convey my greetings, love, to thee.   50
JULIET
    O, think'st thou we shall ever meet again?
ROMEO
    I doubt it not; and all these woes shall serve
    For sweet discourses in our times to come.
⌜JULIET⌝
    O God, I have an ill-divining soul!
    Methinks I see thee, now thou art so low,   55
    As one dead in the bottom of a tomb.
    Either my eyesight fails or thou lookest pale.
ROMEO
    And trust me, love, in my eye so do you.
    Dry sorrow drinks our blood. Adieu, adieu.   *He exits.*

60. **fickle:** inconstant, changeable

62. **faith:** constancy

67. **not down:** not yet in bed

68. **procures:** i.e., brings

76. **shows . . . wit:** always manifests a lack of intelligence

77. **feeling:** strongly felt

Fortune's wheel. (3.5.60)
From Guido delle Colonne, *The hystorye, sege and dystruccyon of Troye,* trans. John Lydgate (1513).

JULIET
O Fortune, Fortune, all men call thee fickle.   60
If thou art fickle, what dost thou with him
That is renowned for faith? Be fickle, Fortune,
For then I hope thou wilt not keep him long,
But send him back.

Enter ⌜Lady Capulet.⌝

LADY CAPULET   Ho, daughter, are you up?   65
JULIET
Who is 't that calls? It is my lady mother.
Is she not down so late or up so early?
What unaccustomed cause procures her hither?
                       ⌜*Juliet descends.*⌝
LADY CAPULET
Why, how now, Juliet?
JULIET   Madam, I am not well.   70
LADY CAPULET
Evermore weeping for your cousin's death?
What, wilt thou wash him from his grave with tears?
An if thou couldst, thou couldst not make him live.
Therefore have done. Some grief shows much of
    love,   75
But much of grief shows still some want of wit.
JULIET
Yet let me weep for such a feeling loss.
LADY CAPULET
So shall you feel the loss, but not the friend
Which you weep for.
JULIET   Feeling so the loss,   80
I cannot choose but ever weep the friend.
LADY CAPULET
Well, girl, thou weep'st not so much for his death
As that the villain lives which slaughtered him.
JULIET
What villain, madam?

88. **grieve:** (1) incense with anger; (2) afflict with longing (From here to line 107, Juliet's words say what her mother expects her to say of a hated Montague but also say what Juliet truly feels about Romeo.)

90. **reach:** (1) grasp; (2) touch

91. **Would:** I wish that

94. **runagate:** runaway, fugitive

95. **dram:** a small draught (here, of poison)

99. **—dead—:** By suspending this word between dashes, editions since Alexander Pope's (1725) have been able to show Juliet's double meaning. She may be read to say "till I behold him dead," or to say "dead is my poor heart."

100. **kinsman:** (1) Tybalt; (2) Romeo

101. **find out but:** only find out

102. **temper:** (1) mix; (2) dilute and thereby turn it from poison into a sleeping potion

106. **wreak:** (1) avenge; (2) bestow

107. **his body that:** the body of the man who

112. **careful:** full of care (for you)

LADY CAPULET   That same villain, Romeo.   85
JULIET, ⌐*aside*⌐
  Villain and he be many miles asunder.—
  God pardon ⌐him.⌐ I do with all my heart,
  And yet no man like he doth grieve my heart.
LADY CAPULET
  That is because the traitor murderer lives.
JULIET
  Ay, madam, from the reach of these my hands.   90
  Would none but I might venge my cousin's death!
LADY CAPULET
  We will have vengeance for it, fear thou not.
  Then weep no more. I'll send to one in Mantua,
  Where that same banished runagate doth live,
  Shall give him such an unaccustomed dram   95
  That he shall soon keep Tybalt company.
  And then, I hope, thou wilt be satisfied.
JULIET
  Indeed, I never shall be satisfied
  With Romeo till I behold him—dead—
  Is my poor heart, so for a kinsman vexed.   100
  Madam, if you could find out but a man
  To bear a poison, I would temper it,
  That Romeo should, upon receipt thereof,
  Soon sleep in quiet. O, how my heart abhors
  To hear him named and cannot come to him   105
  To wreak the love I bore my cousin
  Upon his body that hath slaughtered him.
LADY CAPULET
  Find thou the means, and I'll find such a man.
  But now I'll tell thee joyful tidings, girl.
JULIET
  And joy comes well in such a needy time.   110
  What are they, beseech your ladyship?
LADY CAPULET
  Well, well, thou hast a careful father, child,

113. **heaviness:** i.e., grief
114. **sorted out:** selected; **sudden day:** i.e., a day that is about to come soon
116. **in happy time:** i.e., how opportune
134. **conduit:** fountain
136. **counterfeits:** imitates; **bark:** small sailboat
141. **Without a sudden calm:** i.e., unless suddenly there's a calm; **overset:** capsize

A criminal drawn on a hurdle to execution. (3.5.160)
From *The life and death of*
Mr. Edmund Geninges priest (1614).

One who, to put thee from thy heaviness,
Hath sorted out a sudden day of joy
That thou expects not, nor I looked not for.   115
JULIET
Madam, in happy time! What day is that?
LADY CAPULET
Marry, my child, early next Thursday morn
The gallant, young, and noble gentleman,
The County Paris, at Saint Peter's Church
Shall happily make thee there a joyful bride.   120
JULIET
Now, by Saint Peter's Church, and Peter too,
He shall not make me there a joyful bride!
I wonder at this haste, that I must wed
Ere he that should be husband comes to woo.
I pray you, tell my lord and father, madam,   125
I will not marry yet, and when I do I swear
It shall be Romeo, whom you know I hate,
Rather than Paris. These are news indeed!
LADY CAPULET
Here comes your father. Tell him so yourself,
And see how he will take it at your hands.   130

Enter Capulet and Nurse.

CAPULET
When the sun sets, the earth doth drizzle dew,
But for the sunset of my brother's son
It rains downright.
How now, a conduit, girl? What, still in tears?
Evermore show'ring? In one little body   135
Thou counterfeits a bark, a sea, a wind.
For still thy eyes, which I may call the sea,
Do ebb and flow with tears; the bark thy body is,
Sailing in this salt flood; the winds thy sighs,
Who, raging with thy tears and they with them,   140
Without a sudden calm, will overset

144. **but . . . thanks:** i.e., she refuses any part in it, saying "No, thank you"

146. **Soft:** i.e., wait a moment; **take me with you:** i.e., let me understand you

148. **count her:** regard herself as

149. **wrought:** produced

150. **bride:** i.e., bridegroom

151. **proud you:** i.e., proud that you

153. **for hate . . . love:** i.e., for what I hate when it is intended as love

154. **Chopped logic:** quibbling

156. **minion:** darling (here, a contemptuous term)

158. **fettle:** prepare; **'gainst:** in preparation for

160. **hurdle:** a wooden frame on which criminals were drawn through the streets to execution

161. **green-sickness:** a form of anemia thought to affect girls in puberty, making them pale; **carrion:** a term of contempt (literally, dead flesh); **baggage:** good-for-nothing woman

162. **tallow:** animal fat used in candles (another reference to Juliet's pale face)

Thy tempest-tossèd body.—How now, wife?
Have you delivered to her our decree?

LADY CAPULET
Ay, sir, but she will none, she ⌈gives⌉ you thanks.
I would the fool were married to her grave.   145

CAPULET
Soft, take me with you, take me with you, wife.
How, will she none? Doth she not give us thanks?
Is she not proud? Doth she not count her blessed,
Unworthy as she is, that we have wrought
So worthy a gentleman to be her bride?   150

JULIET
Not proud you have, but thankful that you have.
Proud can I never be of what I hate,
But thankful even for hate that is meant love.

CAPULET
How, how, how, how? Chopped logic? What is this?
"Proud," and "I thank you," and "I thank you not,"   155
And yet "not proud"? Mistress minion you,
Thank me no thankings, nor proud me no prouds,
But fettle your fine joints 'gainst Thursday next
To go with Paris to Saint Peter's Church,
Or I will drag thee on a hurdle thither.   160
Out, you green-sickness carrion! Out, you baggage!
You tallow face!

LADY CAPULET   Fie, fie, what, are you mad?

JULIET, ⌈*kneeling*⌉
Good father, I beseech you on my knees,
Hear me with patience but to speak a word.   165

CAPULET
Hang thee, young baggage, disobedient wretch!
I tell thee what: get thee to church o' Thursday,
Or never after look me in the face.
Speak not; reply not; do not answer me.
My fingers itch.—Wife, we scarce thought us   170
  blessed

175. **hilding:** good-for-nothing

177. **to blame:** blameworthy, deserving rebuke; **rate:** berate, scold

179. **smatter:** chatter

181. **God 'i' g' eden:** exclamation of annoyance (literally, God give you good evening)

184. **gravity:** serious remarks (said contemptuously)

187. **God's bread:** i.e., the sacrament of communion (a strong oath)

188. **tide:** season

189. **still:** always, constantly

192. **demesnes:** property; **nobly ligned:** i.e., noble by lineal descent, by birth

193. **parts:** qualities

195. **puling:** feebly wailing

196. **mammet:** doll; **in her fortune's tender:** i.e., when she is offered (tendered) good fortune

201. **do not use:** am not accustomed

202. **advise:** ponder, consider

That God had lent us but this only child,
But now I see this one is one too much,
And that we have a curse in having her.
Out on her, hilding.   175
NURSE   God in heaven bless her!
  You are to blame, my lord, to rate her so.
CAPULET
  And why, my Lady Wisdom? Hold your tongue.
  Good Prudence, smatter with your gossips, go.
NURSE
  I speak no treason.   180
⌜CAPULET⌝   O, God 'i' g' eden!
⌜NURSE⌝
  May not one speak?
CAPULET   Peace, you mumbling fool!
  Utter your gravity o'er a gossip's bowl,
  For here we need it not.   185
LADY CAPULET
  You are too hot.
CAPULET   God's bread, it makes me mad.
  Day, night, hour, tide, time, work, play,
  Alone, in company, still my care hath been
  To have her matched. And having now provided   190
  A gentleman of noble parentage,
  Of fair demesnes, youthful, and nobly ⌜ligned,⌝
  Stuffed, as they say, with honorable parts,
  Proportioned as one's thought would wish a man—
  And then to have a wretched puling fool,   195
  A whining mammet, in her fortune's tender,
  To answer "I'll not wed. I cannot love.
  I am too young. I pray you, pardon me."
  But, an you will not wed, I'll pardon you!
  Graze where you will, you shall not house with me.   200
  Look to 't; think on 't. I do not use to jest.
  Thursday is near. Lay hand on heart; advise.
  An you be mine, I'll give you to my friend.

207. **bethink you:** reflect seriously; **I'll not be forsworn:** i.e., I'll not take back my words

217. **on earth:** i.e., alive

220. **By leaving earth:** by dying (She has vowed to be his wife until death parts them.)

221–22. **practice stratagems/Upon:** set traps for

226. **all the world to nothing:** i.e., I would bet all against nothing

227. **challenge:** claim

232. **dishclout:** dishrag

233. **quick:** lively

An you be not, hang, beg, starve, die in the streets,
For, by my soul, I'll ne'er acknowledge thee,   205
Nor what is mine shall never do thee good.
Trust to 't; bethink you. I'll not be forsworn.
                                              He exits.

JULIET
Is there no pity sitting in the clouds
That sees into the bottom of my grief?—
O sweet my mother, cast me not away.   210
Delay this marriage for a month, a week,
Or, if you do not, make the bridal bed
In that dim monument where Tybalt lies.

LADY CAPULET
Talk not to me, for I'll not speak a word.
Do as thou wilt, for I have done with thee.   215
                                              She exits.

JULIET, ⌜*rising*⌝
O God! O Nurse, how shall this be prevented?
My husband is on earth, my faith in heaven.
How shall that faith return again to earth
Unless that husband send it me from heaven
By leaving earth? Comfort me; counsel me.—   220
Alack, alack, that heaven should practice stratagems
Upon so soft a subject as myself.—
What sayst thou? Hast thou not a word of joy?
Some comfort, Nurse.

NURSE   Faith, here it is.   225
Romeo is banished, and all the world to nothing
That he dares ne'er come back to challenge you,
Or, if he do, it needs must be by stealth.
Then, since the case so stands as now it doth,
I think it best you married with the County.   230
O, he's a lovely gentleman!
Romeo's a dishclout to him. An eagle, madam,
Hath not so green, so quick, so fair an eye
As Paris hath. Beshrew my very heart,

237–38. **'twere . . . him:** i.e., he is as good as dead since you live here (rather than with him) and have no use of him

240. **both:** i.e., heart and soul

241. **Amen:** Juliet's "Amen" transforms the Nurse's **beshrew** into a solemn curse.

246. **absolved:** forgiven (be given absolution)

248. **Ancient damnation:** old damned one

249. **thus forsworn:** i.e., to break my marriage vows to Romeo

251. **above compare:** beyond comparison

253. **bosom:** i.e., secrets; **twain:** separate

255. **myself:** I

I think you are happy in this second match,   235
For it excels your first, or, if it did not,
Your first is dead, or 'twere as good he were
As living here and you no use of him.

JULIET
Speak'st thou from thy heart?

NURSE
And from my soul too, else beshrew them both.   240

JULIET   Amen.

NURSE   What?

JULIET
Well, thou hast comforted me marvelous much.
Go in and tell my lady I am gone,
Having displeased my father, to Lawrence' cell   245
To make confession and to be absolved.

NURSE
Marry, I will; and this is wisely done.   ⌜*She exits.*⌝

JULIET
Ancient damnation, O most wicked fiend!
Is it more sin to wish me thus forsworn
Or to dispraise my lord with that same tongue   250
Which she hath praisèd him with above compare
So many thousand times? Go, counselor.
Thou and my bosom henceforth shall be twain.
I'll to the Friar to know his remedy.
If all else fail, myself have power to die.   255

She exits.

The Tragedy of

ROMEO
AND
JULIET

ACT 4

4.1 Paris is talking with Friar Lawrence about the coming wedding when Juliet arrives. After Paris leaves, she threatens suicide if Friar Lawrence cannot save her from marrying Paris. Friar Lawrence gives her a potion that will make her appear as if dead the morning of the wedding. He assures her that when she awakes in the vault, Romeo will be there to take her away.

---

2. **father:** i.e., prospective father-in-law

3. **nothing . . . haste:** perhaps, not in the least hesitant myself, lest I slow him down

7. **talk of:** conversation about

8. **Venus:** goddess of love

10. **That . . . sway:** i.e., that she lets her sorrow master her

11. **marriage:** pronounced as a three-syllable word

13–14. **Which . . . society:** i.e., her tears, to which she is too much disposed (**minded**) when she is alone, may be driven away by company (**society**)

⌈ACT 4⌉

⌈Scene 1⌉

Enter Friar ⌈Lawrence⌉ and County Paris.

FRIAR LAWRENCE
  On Thursday, sir? The time is very short.
PARIS
  My father Capulet will have it so,
  And I am nothing slow to slack his haste.
FRIAR LAWRENCE
  You say you do not know the lady's mind?
  Uneven is the course. I like it not.   5
PARIS
  Immoderately she weeps for Tybalt's death,
  And therefore have I little talk of love,
  For Venus smiles not in a house of tears.
  Now, sir, her father counts it dangerous
  That she do give her sorrow so much sway,   10
  And in his wisdom hastes our marriage
  To stop the inundation of her tears,
  Which, too much minded by herself alone,
  May be put from her by society.
  Now do you know the reason of this haste.   15
FRIAR LAWRENCE, ⌈*aside*⌉
  I would I knew not why it should be slowed.—
  Look, sir, here comes the lady toward my cell.

Enter Juliet.

177

18. **Happily:** fortunately
24. **I should confess:** i.e., I would be confessing
28. **price:** value
33. **report:** statement

PARIS
Happily met, my lady and my wife.
JULIET
That may be, sir, when I may be a wife.
PARIS
That "may be" must be, love, on Thursday next.   20
JULIET
What must be shall be.
FRIAR LAWRENCE   That's a certain text.
PARIS
Come you to make confession to this father?
JULIET
To answer that, I should confess to you.
PARIS
Do not deny to him that you love me.   25
JULIET
I will confess to you that I love him.
PARIS
So will you, I am sure, that you love me.
JULIET
If I do so, it will be of more price,
Being spoke behind your back, than to your face.
PARIS
Poor soul, thy face is much abused with tears.   30
JULIET
The tears have got small victory by that,
For it was bad enough before their spite.
PARIS
Thou wrong'st it more than tears with that report.
JULIET
That is no slander, sir, which is a truth,
And what I spake, I spake it to my face.   35
PARIS
Thy face is mine, and thou hast slandered it.
JULIET
It may be so, for it is not mine own.—

40. **pensive:** sorrowful, sad

41. **entreat:** ask for

42. **shield:** prevent that

43. **rouse you:** awaken you (with music, as was customary on the wedding day)

46. **past care:** past being taken care of; past any concern for taking care of myself (Many texts follow the First Quarto and print "past cure.")

48. **strains . . . wits:** forces me beyond the limits of my ingenuity

49. **prorogue:** postpone

54. **Do thou but call:** only call

57–58. **sealed . . . label . . . deed:** A label was a strip of parchment that attached a seal to a deed. **deed:** a legal document or contract

60. **this:** i.e., the knife; **both:** hand and heart

62. **present counsel:** immediate advice

63. **extremes:** extreme difficulties

65. **commission:** authority; **art:** learning

66. **issue . . . honor:** i.e., honorable conclusion

Are you at leisure, holy Father, now,
Or shall I come to you at evening Mass?
FRIAR LAWRENCE
My leisure serves me, pensive daughter, now.—   40
My lord, we must entreat the time alone.
PARIS
God shield I should disturb devotion!—
Juliet, on Thursday early will I rouse you.
Till then, adieu, and keep this holy kiss.   *He exits.*
JULIET
O, shut the door, and when thou hast done so,   45
Come weep with me, past hope, past care, past help.
FRIAR LAWRENCE
O Juliet, I already know thy grief.
It strains me past the compass of my wits.
I hear thou must, and nothing may prorogue it,
On Thursday next be married to this County.   50
JULIET
Tell me not, Friar, that thou hearest of this,
Unless thou tell me how I may prevent it.
If in thy wisdom thou canst give no help,
Do thou but call my resolution wise,
And with this knife I'll help it presently.   55
          ⌈*She shows him her knife.*⌉
God joined my heart and Romeo's, thou our hands;
And ere this hand, by thee to Romeo's sealed,
Shall be the label to another deed,
Or my true heart with treacherous revolt
Turn to another, this shall slay them both.   60
Therefore out of thy long-experienced time
Give me some present counsel, or, behold,
'Twixt my extremes and me this bloody knife
Shall play the umpire, arbitrating that
Which the commission of thy years and art   65
Could to no issue of true honor bring.
Be not so long to speak. I long to die
If what thou speak'st speak not of remedy.

69. **Hold:** stop, wait

70. **craves . . . execution:** demands as reckless action

71. **As . . . desperate:** as that action is unbearable

74. **is it:** i.e., it is

76. **That . . . it:** i.e., you who would meet death itself in order to escape this shame

80. **thievish ways:** roads infested with thieves

82. **charnel house:** house for storing the bones of the dead

83. **O'ercovered quite:** entirely covered up

84. **reeky:** reeking; **chapless:** jawless

86. **hide me:** i.e., hide

95. **being then:** once you are

96. **distilling:** (1) distilled; (2) infusing (the body); **liquor:** liquid

99. **native:** natural; **surcease:** cease

A charnel house. (4.1.82)
From Richard Day, *A booke of Christian prayers* (1590).

FRIAR LAWRENCE
  Hold, daughter, I do spy a kind of hope,
  Which craves as desperate an execution   70
  As that is desperate which we would prevent.
  If, rather than to marry County Paris,
  Thou hast the strength of will to ⌜slay⌝ thyself,
  Then is it likely thou wilt undertake
  A thing like death to chide away this shame,   75
  That cop'st with death himself to 'scape from it;
  And if thou darest, I'll give thee remedy.
JULIET
  O, bid me leap, rather than marry Paris,
  From off the battlements of any tower,
  Or walk in thievish ways, or bid me lurk   80
  Where serpents are. Chain me with roaring bears,
  Or hide me nightly in a charnel house,
  O'ercovered quite with dead men's rattling bones,
  With reeky shanks and yellow ⌜chapless⌝ skulls.
  Or bid me go into a new-made grave   85
  And hide me with a dead man in his ⌜shroud⌝
  (Things that to hear them told have made me
      tremble),
  And I will do it without fear or doubt,
  To live an unstained wife to my sweet love.   90
FRIAR LAWRENCE
  Hold, then. Go home; be merry; give consent
  To marry Paris. Wednesday is tomorrow.
  Tomorrow night look that thou lie alone;
  Let not the Nurse lie with thee in thy chamber.
                     ⌜*Holding out a vial.*⌝
  Take thou this vial, being then in bed,   95
  And this distilling liquor drink thou off;
  When presently through all thy veins shall run
  A cold and drowsy humor; for no pulse
  Shall keep his native progress, but surcease.
  No warmth, no ⌜breath⌝ shall testify thou livest.   100

102. **paly:** pale
104. **supple government:** flexibility
105. **stark:** rigid
112. **uncovered:** bare-faced
115. **against:** in preparation for the time at which
116. **drift:** purpose
121. **inconstant toy:** whim that interferes with your firmness of purpose
122. **Abate:** lessen
127–28. **help afford:** provide help

The roses in thy lips and cheeks shall fade
To ⌜paly⌝ ashes, thy eyes' windows fall
Like death when he shuts up the day of life.
Each part, deprived of supple government,
Shall, stiff and stark and cold, appear like death,   105
And in this borrowed likeness of shrunk death
Thou shalt continue two and forty hours
And then awake as from a pleasant sleep.
Now, when the bridegroom in the morning comes
To rouse thee from thy bed, there art thou dead.   110
Then, as the manner of our country is,
⌜In⌝ thy best robes uncovered on the bier
Thou ⌜shalt⌝ be borne to that same ancient vault
Where all the kindred of the Capulets lie.
In the meantime, against thou shalt awake,   115
Shall Romeo by my letters know our drift,
And hither shall he come, and he and I
Will watch thy ⌜waking,⌝ and that very night
Shall Romeo bear thee hence to Mantua.
And this shall free thee from this present shame,   120
If no inconstant toy nor womanish fear
Abate thy valor in the acting it.

JULIET
Give me, give me! O, tell not me of fear!

FRIAR LAWRENCE, ⌜*giving Juliet the vial*⌝
Hold, get you gone. Be strong and prosperous
In this resolve. I'll send a friar with speed   125
To Mantua with my letters to thy lord.

JULIET
Love give me strength, and strength shall help
    afford.
Farewell, dear Father.
                ⌜*They*⌝ *exit* ⌜*in different directions.*⌝

4.2 Capulet energetically directs preparations for Juliet's wedding. When she returns from Friar Lawrence and pretends to have learned obedience, Capulet is so delighted that he moves the wedding up to the next day and goes off to tell Paris the new date.

———

0 SD. **Servingmen, two or three:** i.e., two or three servingmen

2. **cunning:** skilled

3. **none ill:** no incompetent ones; **try:** test (to see)

6–7. **'tis . . . fingers:** proverbial

10. **unfurnished:** unprovided

14. **peevish:** obstinate; **harlotry:** good-for-nothing (often—but probably not here—with reference to a harlot, or whore); **it:** i.e., she

18. **learned me:** i.e., learned

⌜Scene 2⌝

Enter Father Capulet, Mother, Nurse, and Servingmen,
two or three.

CAPULET
So many guests invite as here are writ.
                    ⌜*One or two of the Servingmen exit*
                              with Capulet's list.⌝
Sirrah, go hire me twenty cunning cooks.

SERVINGMAN   You shall have none ill, sir, for I'll try if
they can lick their fingers.

CAPULET   How canst thou try them so?   5

SERVINGMAN   Marry, sir, 'tis an ill cook that cannot lick
his own fingers. Therefore he that cannot lick his
fingers goes not with me.

CAPULET   Go, begone.   ⌜*Servingman exits.*⌝
We shall be much unfurnished for this time.—   10
What, is my daughter gone to Friar Lawrence?

NURSE   Ay, forsooth.

CAPULET
Well, he may chance to do some good on her.
A peevish ⌜self-willed⌝ harlotry it is.

Enter Juliet.

NURSE
See where she comes from shrift with merry look.   15

CAPULET
How now, my headstrong, where have you been
gadding?

JULIET
Where I have learned me to repent the sin
Of disobedient opposition
To you and your behests, and am enjoined   20
By holy Lawrence to fall prostrate here   ⌜*Kneeling.*⌝
To beg your pardon. Pardon, I beseech you.
Henceforward I am ever ruled by you.

25. **this knot:** the marriage of Juliet and Paris
27. **becomèd:** fitting, becoming
29. **on 't:** of it
33. **bound:** obliged
34. **closet:** private room
35–36. **sort . . . furnish me:** select such clothes as you think suitable for me to wear
48. **Against:** in preparation for

CAPULET
    Send for the County. Go tell him of this.
    I'll have this knot knit up tomorrow morning.   25
JULIET
    I met the youthful lord at Lawrence' cell
    And gave him what becomèd love I might,
    Not stepping o'er the bounds of modesty.
CAPULET
    Why, I am glad on 't. This is well. Stand up.
                                   ⌜*Juliet rises.*⌝
    This is as 't should be.—Let me see the County.   30
    Ay, marry, go, I say, and fetch him hither.—
    Now, afore God, this reverend holy friar,
    All our whole city is much bound to him.
JULIET
    Nurse, will you go with me into my closet
    To help me sort such needful ornaments   35
    As you think fit to furnish me tomorrow?
LADY CAPULET
    No, not till Thursday. There is time enough.
CAPULET
    Go, Nurse. Go with her. We'll to church tomorrow.
                           ⌜*Juliet and the Nurse*⌝ *exit.*
LADY CAPULET
    We shall be short in our provision.
    'Tis now near night.   40
CAPULET   Tush, I will stir about,
    And all things shall be well, I warrant thee, wife.
    Go thou to Juliet. Help to deck up her.
    I'll not to bed tonight. Let me alone.
    I'll play the housewife for this once.—What ho!—   45
    They are all forth. Well, I will walk myself
    To County Paris, to prepare up him
    Against tomorrow. My heart is wondrous light
    Since this same wayward girl is so reclaimed.
                                   ⌜*They*⌝ *exit.*

4.3 Juliet sends the Nurse away for the night. After facing her terror at the prospect of awaking in her family's burial vault, Juliet drinks the potion that Friar Lawrence has given her.

------

  1. **those attires:** this apparel
  4. **state:** condition
  5. **cross:** full of contradictions
  7. **culled:** chosen
  7–8. **necessaries . . . behooveful:** i.e., necessary and useful things
  8. **state:** display

⌜Scene 3⌝
Enter Juliet and Nurse.

JULIET
Ay, those attires are best. But, gentle Nurse,
I pray thee leave me to myself tonight,
For I have need of many orisons
To move the heavens to smile upon my state,
Which, well thou knowest, is cross and full of sin.   5

Enter ⌜Lady Capulet.⌝

LADY CAPULET
What, are you busy, ho? Need you my help?
JULIET
No, madam, we have culled such necessaries
As are behooveful for our state tomorrow.
So please you, let me now be left alone,
And let the Nurse this night sit up with you,   10
For I am sure you have your hands full all
In this so sudden business.
LADY CAPULET   Good night.
Get thee to bed and rest, for thou hast need.
                    ⌜*Lady Capulet and the Nurse*⌝ *exit.*
JULIET
Farewell.—God knows when we shall meet again.   15
I have a faint cold fear thrills through my veins
That almost freezes up the heat of life.
I'll call them back again to comfort me.—
Nurse!—What should she do here?
My dismal scene I needs must act alone.   20
Come, vial.   ⌜*She takes out the vial.*⌝
What if this mixture do not work at all?
Shall I be married then tomorrow morning?
                    ⌜*She takes out her knife
                    and puts it down beside her.*⌝
No, no, this shall forbid it. Lie thou there.
What if it be a poison which the Friar   25

26. **Subtly:** craftily; **ministered:** provided
29. **should not:** i.e., should not be
30. **still been tried:** always been proved to be
36. **strangled:** suffocated
37. **like:** i.e., likely that
38. **conceit of:** thoughts (or images) of
40. **As:** i.e., as being
43. **green in earth:** freshly interred in the vault
48. **mandrakes:** plants whose forked roots make them resemble the human body, and which were thought to shriek when torn out of the ground
49. **That:** i.e., so that
54. **rage:** madness; **great kinsman:** e.g., great-grandfather or great-uncle
57. **spit:** impale
58. **Stay:** wait

A mandrake. (4.3.48)
From Rembert Dodoens, *Purgantium aliarumque* (1574).

Subtly hath ministered to have me dead,
Lest in this marriage he should be dishonored
Because he married me before to Romeo?
I fear it is. And yet methinks it should not,
For he hath still been tried a holy man.   30
How if, when I am laid into the tomb,
I wake before the time that Romeo
Come to redeem me? There's a fearful point.
Shall I not then be stifled in the vault,
To whose foul mouth no healthsome air breathes in,   35
And there die strangled ere my Romeo comes?
Or, if I live, is it not very like
The horrible conceit of death and night,
Together with the terror of the place—
As in a vault, an ancient receptacle   40
Where for this many hundred years the bones
Of all my buried ancestors are packed;
Where bloody Tybalt, yet but green in earth,
Lies fest'ring in his shroud; where, as they say,
At some hours in the night spirits resort—   45
Alack, alack, is it not like that I,
So early waking, what with loathsome smells,
And shrieks like mandrakes torn out of the earth,
That living mortals, hearing them, run mad—
O, if I ⌐wake,⌐ shall I not be distraught,   50
Environèd with all these hideous fears,
And madly play with my forefathers' joints,
And pluck the mangled Tybalt from his shroud,
And, in this rage, with some great kinsman's bone,
As with a club, dash out my desp'rate brains?   55
O look, methinks I see my cousin's ghost
Seeking out Romeo that did spit his body
Upon a rapier's point! Stay, Tybalt, stay!
Romeo, Romeo, Romeo! Here's drink. I drink to
    thee.   ⌐*She drinks and falls upon her bed*   60
                              within the curtains.⌐

4.4 The Capulets and the Nurse stay up all night to get ready for the wedding. Capulet, hearing Paris approach with musicians, orders the Nurse to awaken Juliet.

---

2. **pastry:** room where pastry is made
3. **second cock hath crowed:** i.e., it is after 3 A.M. (Conventionally, the cock crowed first at midnight, then at 3 A.M., and then one hour before daybreak.)
5. **baked meats:** meat pies
7. **cot-quean:** i.e., a man who meddles in women's kitchen tasks (Some editors assign this speech to Lady Capulet on the grounds that the Nurse would not be free to speak to Capulet in this way.)
9. **For:** because of; **watching:** staying awake
12. **mouse-hunt:** i.e., chaser of women (literally, a mouse-hunter like a cat or weasel)
13. **watch . . . watching:** keep you in sight in order to prevent you from "mouse-hunting"
14. **jealous hood:** i.e., probably, jealous woman (otherwise unexplained)

⌜Scene 4⌝
Enter ⌜Lady Capulet⌝ and Nurse.

LADY CAPULET
  Hold, take these keys, and fetch more spices, Nurse.
NURSE
  They call for dates and quinces in the pastry.

Enter old Capulet.

CAPULET
  Come, stir, stir, stir! The second cock hath crowed.
  The curfew bell hath rung. 'Tis three o'clock.—
  Look to the baked meats, good Angelica.   5
  Spare not for cost.
NURSE   Go, you cot-quean, go,
  Get you to bed. Faith, you'll be sick tomorrow
  For this night's watching.
CAPULET
  No, not a whit. What, I have watched ere now   10
  All night for lesser cause, and ne'er been sick.
LADY CAPULET
  Ay, you have been a mouse-hunt in your time,
  But I will watch you from such watching now.
                    Lady ⌜Capulet⌝ and Nurse exit.
CAPULET
  A jealous hood, a jealous hood!

*Enter three or four ⌜Servingmen⌝ with spits and logs
          and baskets.*

                    Now fellow,   15
  What is there?
⌜FIRST SERVINGMAN⌝
  Things for the cook, sir, but I know not what.
CAPULET
  Make haste, make haste.   ⌜*First Servingman exits.*⌝
                    Sirrah, fetch drier logs.
  Call Peter. He will show thee where they are.   20

23. **Mass:** i.e., by the Mass; **whoreson:** literally, whore's son, but here only a kind of familiar address

24. **loggerhead:** blockhead

26. **straight:** straightway, immediately

29. **trim:** dress

4.5 The Nurse finds Juliet in the deathlike trance caused by the Friar's potion and announces Juliet's death. Juliet's parents and Paris join the Nurse in lamentation. Friar Lawrence interrupts them and begins to arrange Juliet's funeral. The scene closes with an exchange of wordplay between Capulet's servant Peter and Paris's musicians.

1. **Fast:** i.e., fast asleep

5. **pennyworths:** little bits (of sleep)

8. **set up his rest:** firmly decided (with a sexual implication for which the Nurse then asks forgiveness, only to introduce further sexual implications with "take" [line 12] and "fright you up" [line 13])

10. **Marry:** by the Virgin Mary

⌜SECOND SERVINGMAN⌝
 I have a head, sir, that will find out logs
 And never trouble Peter for the matter.
CAPULET
 Mass, and well said. A merry whoreson, ha!
 Thou shalt be loggerhead.
                              ⌜*Second Servingman exits.*⌝
                    Good ⌜faith,⌝ 'tis day.   25
 The County will be here with music straight,
                                    Play music.
 For so he said he would. I hear him near.—
 Nurse!—Wife! What ho!—What, Nurse, I say!

                   Enter Nurse.

 Go waken Juliet. Go and trim her up.
 I'll go and chat with Paris. Hie, make haste,   30
 Make haste. The bridegroom he is come already.
 Make haste, I say.
                              ⌜*He exits.*⌝

                   ⌜Scene 5⌝

NURSE, ⌜*approaching the bed*⌝
 Mistress! What, mistress! Juliet!—Fast, I warrant
   her, she.—
 Why, lamb, why, lady! Fie, you slugabed!
 Why, love, I say! Madam! Sweetheart! Why, bride!—
 What, not a word?—You take your pennyworths   5
   now.
 Sleep for a week, for the next night, I warrant,
 The County Paris hath set up his rest
 That you shall rest but little.—God forgive me,
 Marry, and amen! How sound is she asleep!   10
 I needs must wake her.—Madam, madam, madam!
 Ay, let the County take you in your bed,

13. **Will . . . be?:** i.e., won't you wake up
18. **weraday:** exclamation of sorrow
19. **aqua vitae:** strong drink, usually brandy
23. **heavy:** sorrowful
30. **Out, alas:** expressions of sorrow

Mourners with corpse on bier. (4.5)
From Tommaso Porcacchi, *Funerali antichi* (1591).

He'll fright you up, i' faith.—Will it not be?
⌐*She opens the bed's curtains.*⌐
What, dressed, and in your clothes, and down
   again?   15
I must needs wake you. Lady, lady, lady!—
Alas, alas! Help, help! My lady's dead.—
O, weraday, that ever I was born!—
Some aqua vitae, ho!—My lord! My lady!

⌐*Enter Lady Capulet.*⌐

LADY CAPULET
  What noise is here?   20
NURSE   O lamentable day!
LADY CAPULET
  What is the matter?
NURSE   Look, look!—O heavy day!
LADY CAPULET
  O me! O me! My child, my only life.
  Revive, look up, or I will die with thee.   25
  Help, help! Call help.

Enter ⌐*Capulet.*⌐

CAPULET
  For shame, bring Juliet forth. Her lord is come.
NURSE
  She's dead, deceased. She's dead, alack the day!
LADY CAPULET
  Alack the day, she's dead, she's dead, she's dead.
CAPULET
  Ha, let me see her! Out, alas, she's cold.   30
  Her blood is settled, and her joints are stiff.
  Life and these lips have long been separated.
  Death lies on her like an untimely frost
  Upon the sweetest flower of all the field.
NURSE
  O lamentable day!   35

43. **deflowerèd by him:** i.e., sexually visited by Death

46. **living:** livelihood

47. **thought long to see:** i.e., long looked forward to seeing (From this line to the Friar's interruption at line 71, four characters each have a half-dozen lines of laments over Juliet's "death." It has been suggested that the four ought to deliver their lines simultaneously, as may just possibly be indicated by this stage direction in the First Quarto: "All at once cry out and wring their hands.")

49. **unhappy:** disastrous

51. **lasting:** everlasting

54. **catched:** snatched

61. **Beguiled:** disappointed, cheated

LADY CAPULET   O woeful time!
CAPULET
  Death, that hath ta'en her hence to make me wail,
  Ties up my tongue and will not let me speak.

  Enter Friar ⌈Lawrence⌉ and the County ⌈Paris, with
  Musicians.⌉

FRIAR LAWRENCE
  Come, is the bride ready to go to church?
CAPULET
  Ready to go, but never to return.—   40
  O son, the night before thy wedding day
  Hath death lain with thy wife. There she lies,
  Flower as she was, deflowerèd by him.
  Death is my son-in-law; death is my heir.
  My daughter he hath wedded. I will die   45
  And leave him all. Life, living, all is death's.
PARIS
  Have I thought ⌈long⌉ to see this morning's face,
  And doth it give me such a sight as this?
LADY CAPULET
  Accursed, unhappy, wretched, hateful day!
  Most miserable hour that e'er time saw   50
  In lasting labor of his pilgrimage!
  But one, poor one, one poor and loving child,
  But one thing to rejoice and solace in,
  And cruel death hath catched it from my sight!
NURSE
  O woe, O woeful, woeful, woeful day!   55
  Most lamentable day, most woeful day
  That ever, ever I did yet behold!
  O day, O day, O day, O hateful day!
  Never was seen so black a day as this!
  O woeful day, O woeful day!   60
PARIS
  Beguiled, divorcèd, wrongèd, spited, slain!

66. **Uncomfortable:** causing discomfort
67. **solemnity:** festival (Juliet's wedding)
71. **Confusion:** ruin
72. **confusions:** outbursts, commotions
73. **Had part:** i.e., each had a share
77. **her promotion:** her material advancement
81. **ill:** badly
82. **she is well:** i.e., she is happy in heaven ("She is well" was a phrase indicating that someone had died.)
85. **rosemary:** an aromatic plant, symbol of remembrance (associated with both funerals and weddings)
88. **fond:** foolish
89. **reason's merriment:** i.e., cause for reason's rejoicing
90. **ordainèd festival:** planned to be festive
91. **office:** function
93. **cheer:** food and drink
94. **sullen dirges:** mournful funeral songs

Most detestable death, by thee beguiled,
By cruel, cruel thee quite overthrown!
O love! O life! Not life, but love in death!

CAPULET
Despised, distressèd, hated, martyred, killed!   65
Uncomfortable time, why cam'st thou now
To murder, murder our solemnity?
O child! O child! My soul and not my child!
Dead art thou! Alack, my child is dead,
And with my child my joys are burièd.   70

FRIAR LAWRENCE
Peace, ho, for shame! Confusion's ⌜cure⌝ lives not
In these confusions. Heaven and yourself
Had part in this fair maid. Now heaven hath all,
And all the better is it for the maid.
Your part in her you could not keep from death,   75
But heaven keeps his part in eternal life.
The most you sought was her promotion,
For 'twas your heaven she should be advanced;
And weep you now, seeing she is advanced
Above the clouds, as high as heaven itself?   80
O, in this love you love your child so ill
That you run mad, seeing that she is well.
She's not well married that lives married long,
But she's best married that dies married young.
Dry up your tears, and stick your rosemary   85
On this fair corse, and, as the custom is,
And in her best array, bear her to church,
For though ⌜fond⌝ nature bids us all lament,
Yet nature's tears are reason's merriment.

CAPULET
All things that we ordainèd festival   90
Turn from their office to black funeral:
Our instruments to melancholy bells,
Our wedding cheer to a sad burial feast,
Our solemn hymns to sullen dirges change,

100. **lour:** frown

101. **Move:** provoke

102. **put up:** i.e., put away

104. **case:** event

105. **the case may be amended:** (1) the situation might be improved; (2) the case in which I keep my instrument might be mended

106. **"Heart's ease":** the name of a popular song

110–11. **"My heart is full":** part of a line from a popular song

111. **merry dump:** a contradiction in terms, since a **dump** is a sad song

119. **gleek:** jest, jeer

119–20. **give you the minstrel:** call you a minstrel

Our bridal flowers serve for a buried corse,   95
And all things change them to the contrary.
FRIAR LAWRENCE
Sir, go you in, and, madam, go with him,
And go, Sir Paris. Everyone prepare
To follow this fair corse unto her grave.
The heavens do lour upon you for some ill.   100
Move them no more by crossing their high will.
⌐*All but the Nurse and the Musicians*¬ *exit.*
⌐FIRST MUSICIAN¬
Faith, we may put up our pipes and be gone.
NURSE
Honest good fellows, ah, put up, put up,
For, well you know, this is a pitiful case.
⌐FIRST MUSICIAN¬
Ay, ⌐by¬ my troth, the case may be amended.   105
⌐*Nurse*¬ *exits.*

Enter ⌐*Peter.*¬

PETER Musicians, O musicians, "Heart's ease,"
"Heart's ease." O, an you will have me live, play
"Heart's ease."
⌐FIRST MUSICIAN¬ Why "Heart's ease"?
PETER O musicians, because my heart itself plays "My   110
heart is full." O, play me some merry dump to
comfort me.
⌐FIRST MUSICIAN¬ Not a dump, we. 'Tis no time to play
now.
PETER You will not then?   115
⌐FIRST MUSICIAN¬ No.
PETER I will then give it you soundly.
⌐FIRST MUSICIAN¬ What will you give us?
PETER No money, on my faith, but the gleek. I will give
you the minstrel.   120
⌐FIRST MUSICIAN¬ Then will I give you the serving-
creature.

124. **carry no crochets:** i.e., tolerate none of your whims (**Crochets** also meant quarter notes.); **re, fa:** names of musical notes

125. **note:** pay attention to

128. **put out:** display

129. **have at you:** i.e., I'll attack you

132–34. **When griping . . . sound:** from a song by Richard Edwardes published in 1576   **griping:** distressing **dumps:** low spirits

136. **Catling:** a small catgut string for a fiddle

139. **Prates:** i.e., he just chatters; **Rebeck:** a fiddle

141. **sound:** play

142. **Soundpost:** a peg of wood fixed underneath the bridge of a violin or fiddle

144. **cry you mercy:** i.e., beg your pardon; **say:** i.e., speak, because you can only sing

148. **lend redress:** make amends

149. **this same:** i.e., this man (Peter)

151. **tarry:** wait; **stay:** i.e., stay for

PETER   Then will I lay the serving-creature's dagger on
your pate. I will carry no crochets. I'll *re* you, I'll *fa*
you. Do you note me?   125

⌐FIRST MUSICIAN⌐   An you *re* us and *fa* us, you note us.

SECOND ⌐MUSICIAN⌐   Pray you, put up your dagger and
put out your wit.

⌐PETER⌐   Then have at you with my wit. I will dry-beat
you with an iron wit, and put up my iron dagger.   130
Answer me like men.
⌐*Sings.*⌐ *When griping griefs the heart doth wound*
        ⌐*And doleful dumps the mind oppress,*⌐
        Then music with her silver sound—
Why "silver sound"? Why "music with her silver   135
sound"? What say you, Simon Catling?

⌐FIRST MUSICIAN⌐   Marry, sir, because silver hath a
sweet sound.

PETER   Prates.—What say you, Hugh Rebeck?

SECOND ⌐MUSICIAN⌐   I say "silver sound" because musi-   140
cians sound for silver.

PETER   Prates too.—What say you, James Soundpost?

THIRD ⌐MUSICIAN⌐   Faith, I know not what to say.

PETER   O, I cry you mercy. You are the singer. I will say
for you. It is "music with her silver sound" because   145
musicians have no gold for sounding:
⌐*Sings.*⌐   *Then music with her silver sound*
        With speedy help doth lend redress.
                                    He exits.

⌐FIRST MUSICIAN⌐   What a pestilent knave is this same!

SECOND ⌐MUSICIAN⌐   Hang him, Jack. Come, we'll in   150
here, tarry for the mourners, and stay dinner.
                            ⌐*They*⌐ *exit.*

The Tragedy of

ROMEO

AND

JULIET

ACT 5

5.1 Romeo's man, Balthasar, arrives in Mantua with news of Juliet's death. Romeo sends him to hire horses for their immediate return to Verona. Romeo then buys poison so that he can join Juliet in death in the Capulets' burial vault.

---

   1. **trust . . . sleep:** depend on the illusory hopes provided by dreams, as if they were true

   2. **at hand:** soon

   3. **bosom's . . . throne:** i.e., perhaps, love sits lightly in my heart; or, perhaps, my heart sits lightly in my breast

   7. **gives . . . leave:** permits

  12. **shadows:** i.e., images, dreams

⌜ACT 5⌝

⌜Scene 1⌝
Enter Romeo.

ROMEO
 If I may trust the flattering truth of sleep,
 My dreams presage some joyful news at hand.
 My bosom's ⌜lord⌝ sits lightly in his throne,
 And all this day an unaccustomed spirit
 Lifts me above the ground with cheerful thoughts.   5
 I dreamt my lady came and found me dead
 (Strange dream that gives a dead man leave to
   think!)
 And breathed such life with kisses in my lips
 That I revived and was an emperor.   10
 Ah me, how sweet is love itself possessed
 When but love's shadows are so rich in joy!

 Enter Romeo's man ⌜Balthasar, in riding boots.⌝

 News from Verona!—How now, Balthasar?
 Dost thou not bring me letters from the Friar?
 How doth my lady? Is my father well?   15
 How doth my Juliet? That I ask again,
 For nothing can be ill if she be well.
BALTHASAR
 Then she is well and nothing can be ill.
 Her body sleeps in Capels' monument,
 And her immortal part with angels lives.   20

211

22. **presently took post:** immediately departed on a post-horse (See line 27.)

24. **office:** duty

27. **post-horses:** horses kept at inns for the use of travelers

28. **patience:** self-control

29. **import:** portend, forebode

38. **for means:** by what means

40. **apothecary:** druggist

41. **late:** recently

42. **weeds:** clothes; **overwhelming:** jutting?

43. **Culling of simples:** selecting medicinal herbs

45–47. **tortoise . . . fishes:** Other writings of the period suggest that apothecaries decorated their shops with the remains of alligators and such things.

50. **of roses:** made of compressed rose petals

I saw her laid low in her kindred's vault
And presently took post to tell it you.
O, pardon me for bringing these ill news,
Since you did leave it for my office, sir.

ROMEO
Is it e'en so?—Then I ⌜defy⌝ you, stars!— 25
Thou knowest my lodging. Get me ink and paper,
And hire post-horses. I will hence tonight.

BALTHASAR
I do beseech you, sir, have patience.
Your looks are pale and wild and do import
Some misadventure. 30

ROMEO   Tush, thou art deceived.
Leave me, and do the thing I bid thee do.
Hast thou no letters to me from the Friar?

BALTHASAR
No, my good lord.

ROMEO   No matter. Get thee gone, 35
And hire those horses. I'll be with thee straight.
                              ⌜*Balthasar*⌝ *exits.*

Well, Juliet, I will lie with thee tonight.
Let's see for means. O mischief, thou art swift
To enter in the thoughts of desperate men.
I do remember an apothecary 40
(And hereabouts he dwells) which late I noted
In tattered weeds, with overwhelming brows,
Culling of simples. Meager were his looks.
Sharp misery had worn him to the bones.
And in his needy shop a tortoise hung, 45
An alligator stuffed, and other skins
Of ill-shaped fishes; and about his shelves,
A beggarly account of empty boxes,
Green earthen pots, bladders, and musty seeds,
Remnants of packthread, and old cakes of roses 50
Were thinly scattered to make up a show.
Noting this penury, to myself I said

54. **Whose . . . Mantua:** i.e., the sale of which in Mantua is penalized by immediate execution

55. **caitiff:** miserable

63. **ducats:** valuable gold coins

64. **dram:** a small draught; **soon-speeding gear:** quick-working stuff

66. **That:** i.e., so that

67. **trunk:** body

70. **mortal:** deadly

71. **any he:** i.e., anyone; **utters:** sells

74. **Need and oppression:** i.e., oppressive need

75. **Contempt and beggary:** i.e., contemptible beggary

77. **affords:** provides

An apothecary. (5.1.40)
From Ambroise Paré, *The workes of . . .* (1634).

"An if a man did need a poison now,
Whose sale is present death in Mantua,
Here lives a caitiff wretch would sell it him."   55
O, this same thought did but forerun my need,
And this same needy man must sell it me.
As I remember, this should be the house.
Being holiday, the beggar's shop is shut.—
What ho, Apothecary!   60

⌜*Enter Apothecary.*⌝

APOTHECARY   Who calls so loud?
ROMEO
Come hither, man. I see that thou art poor.
⌜*He offers money.*⌝
Hold, there is forty ducats. Let me have
A dram of poison, such soon-speeding gear
As will disperse itself through all the veins,   65
That the life-weary taker may fall dead,
And that the trunk may be discharged of breath
As violently as hasty powder fired
Doth hurry from the fatal cannon's womb.
APOTHECARY
Such mortal drugs I have, but Mantua's law   70
Is death to any he that utters them.
ROMEO
Art thou so bare and full of wretchedness,
And fearest to die? Famine is in thy cheeks,
Need and oppression starveth in thy eyes,
Contempt and beggary hangs upon thy back.   75
The world is not thy friend, nor the world's law.
The world affords no law to make thee rich.
Then be not poor, but break it, and take this.
APOTHECARY
My poverty, but not my will, consents.
ROMEO
I ⌜pay⌝ thy poverty and not thy will.   80

90. **cordial:** invigorating drink

5.2   Friar John enters, bringing with him the letter that he was to have delivered to Romeo. He tells why he was unable to deliver the letter. Friar Lawrence anxiously goes to the tomb to be there when Juliet comes out of her trance.

––––––––––

2. **This same:** i.e., this
5. **Going:** i.e., I, going; **a barefoot brother:** i.e., another Franciscan friar
6. **associate:** accompany
7. **Here:** i.e., who was here
8. **finding:** i.e., I finding; **searchers:** i.e., officials
10. **pestilence:** plague
12. **speed:** i.e., journey

A barefoot brother. (5.2.5)
From Niccolo Catalano, *Fiume del terrestre paradiso* (1652).

216

APOTHECARY, ⌜*giving him the poison*⌝
  Put this in any liquid thing you will
  And drink it off, and if you had the strength
  Of twenty men, it would dispatch you straight.
ROMEO, ⌜*handing him the money*⌝
  There is thy gold, worse poison to men's souls,
  Doing more murder in this loathsome world   85
  Than these poor compounds that thou mayst not
    sell.
  I sell thee poison; thou hast sold me none.
  Farewell, buy food, and get thyself in flesh.
                              ⌜*Apothecary exits.*⌝
  Come, cordial and not poison, go with me   90
  To Juliet's grave, for there must I use thee.
                              ⌜*He exits.*⌝

                    ⌜Scene 2⌝
                Enter Friar John.

FRIAR JOHN
  Holy Franciscan Friar, brother, ho!

              Enter ⌜*Friar*⌝ *Lawrence.*

FRIAR LAWRENCE
  This same should be the voice of Friar John.—
  Welcome from Mantua. What says Romeo?
  Or, if his mind be writ, give me his letter.
FRIAR JOHN
  Going to find a barefoot brother out,   5
  One of our order, to associate me,
  Here in this city visiting the sick,
  And finding him, the searchers of the town,
  Suspecting that we both were in a house
  Where the infectious pestilence did reign,   10
  Sealed up the doors and would not let us forth,
  So that my speed to Mantua there was stayed.

13. **bare:** i.e., bore, carried
17. **my brotherhood:** my vocation as friar
18. **nice:** trivial; **charge:** importance
19. **dear:** precious; dire, costly
21. **crow:** crowbar
27. **accidents:** events, happenings

5.3 Paris visits Juliet's tomb and, when Romeo arrives, challenges him. Romeo and Paris fight and Paris is killed. Romeo then takes poison, dying as he kisses Juliet. As Friar Lawrence enters the tomb, Juliet awakes to find Romeo lying dead. Frightened by a noise, the Friar flees the tomb. Juliet kills herself with Romeo's dagger. Alerted by Paris's page, the watch arrives and finds the bodies. Then the Prince, the Capulets, and Montague arrive. Friar Lawrence gives an account of the marriage of Romeo and Juliet, whose deaths lead Montague and Capulet to declare that their hostility is at an end.

---

1. **aloof:** at a distance
2. **it:** i.e., the torch
3. **lay thee all along:** i.e., stretch out

FRIAR LAWRENCE
  Who bare my letter, then, to Romeo?
FRIAR JOHN
  I could not send it (here it is again)
                    ⌜*Returning the letter.*⌝
  Nor get a messenger to bring it thee,   15
  So fearful were they of infection.
FRIAR LAWRENCE
  Unhappy fortune! By my brotherhood,
  The letter was not nice but full of charge,
  Of dear import, and the neglecting it
  May do much danger. Friar John, go hence.   20
  Get me an iron crow and bring it straight
  Unto my cell.
FRIAR JOHN
  Brother, I'll go and bring it thee.   *He exits.*
FRIAR LAWRENCE
  Now must I to the monument alone.
  Within this three hours will fair Juliet wake.   25
  She will beshrew me much that Romeo
  Hath had no notice of these accidents.
  But I will write again to Mantua,
  And keep her at my cell till Romeo come.
  Poor living corse, closed in a dead man's tomb!   30
                                        He exits.

                    ⌜Scene 3⌝
              Enter Paris and his Page.

PARIS
  Give me thy torch, boy. Hence and stand aloof.
  Yet put it out, for I would not be seen.
  Under yond ⌜yew⌝ trees lay thee all along,
  Holding thy ear close to the hollow ground.
  So shall no foot upon the churchyard tread   5
  (Being loose, unfirm, with digging up of graves)

11. **adventure:** venture, take the risk
14. **sweet:** scented; **dew:** dampen
15. **wanting:** lacking
20. **cross:** impede, thwart
21. **Muffle:** wrap up and thereby hide
22. **wrenching iron:** i.e., crowbar
25. **charge:** command
27. **course:** proceedings
32. **dear:** important
33. **jealous:** suspicious

But thou shalt hear it. Whistle then to me
As signal that thou hearest something approach.
Give me those flowers. Do as I bid thee. Go.

PAGE, ⌜*aside*⌝
I am almost afraid to stand alone　　　　　　　10
Here in the churchyard. Yet I will adventure.
⌜*He moves away from Paris.*⌝

PARIS, ⌜*scattering flowers*⌝
Sweet flower, with flowers thy bridal bed I strew
(O woe, thy canopy is dust and stones!)
Which with sweet water nightly I will dew,
Or, wanting that, with tears distilled by moans.　　15
The obsequies that I for thee will keep
Nightly shall be to strew thy grave and weep.
⌜*Page*⌝ *whistles.*
The boy gives warning something doth approach.
What cursèd foot wanders this way tonight,
To cross my obsequies and true love's rite?　　　20
What, with a torch? Muffle me, night, awhile.
⌜*He steps aside.*⌝

Enter Romeo and ⌜*Balthasar.*⌝

ROMEO
Give me that mattock and the wrenching iron.
Hold, take this letter. Early in the morning
See thou deliver it to my lord and father.
Give me the light. Upon thy life I charge thee,　　25
Whate'er thou hearest or seest, stand all aloof
And do not interrupt me in my course.
Why I descend into this bed of death
Is partly to behold my lady's face,
But chiefly to take thence from her dead finger　30
A precious ring, a ring that I must use
In dear employment. Therefore hence, begone.
But, if thou, jealous, dost return to pry
In what I farther shall intend to do,

39. **empty:** hungry
43. **For all this same:** i.e., all the same
44. **fear:** distrust; **doubt:** suspect
45. **detestable:** accented on the first and third syllables; **maw, womb:** stomach
48. **in despite:** maliciously (because the stomach-tomb is already **gorged**)
52. **villainous shame:** i.e., shameful villainy

By heaven, I will tear thee joint by joint   35
And strew this hungry churchyard with thy limbs.
The time and my intents are savage-wild,
More fierce and more inexorable far
Than empty tigers or the roaring sea.
⌜BALTHASAR⌝
I will be gone, sir, and not trouble you.   40
ROMEO
So shalt thou show me friendship. Take thou that.
⌜*Giving money.*⌝
Live and be prosperous, and farewell, good fellow.
⌜BALTHASAR, *aside*⌝
For all this same, I'll hide me hereabout.
His looks I fear, and his intents I doubt.
⌜*He steps aside.*⌝
ROMEO, ⌜*beginning to force open the tomb*⌝
Thou detestable maw, thou womb of death,   45
Gorged with the dearest morsel of the earth,
Thus I enforce thy rotten jaws to open,
And in despite I'll cram thee with more food.
PARIS
This is that banished haughty Montague
That murdered my love's cousin, with which grief   50
It is supposèd the fair creature died,
And here is come to do some villainous shame
To the dead bodies. I will apprehend him.
⌜*Stepping forward.*⌝
Stop thy unhallowed toil, vile Montague.
Can vengeance be pursued further than death?   55
Condemnèd villain, I do apprehend thee.
Obey and go with me, for thou must die.
ROMEO
I must indeed, and therefore came I hither.
Good gentle youth, tempt not a desp'rate man.
Fly hence and leave me. Think upon these gone.   60
Let them affright thee. I beseech thee, youth,

68. **commination:** threat (This word, first adopted into an edition of *Romeo and Juliet* by G. W. Williams, is in the Church of England's *Book of Common Prayer*, in "A Commination Against Sinners.")

71. **watch:** watchmen, guards

78. **should have:** was to have

83. **triumphant:** glorious

84. **lantern:** a turret with many windows

86. **feasting presence:** chamber where a monarch would entertain

A lantern. (5.3.84)
From Sebastiano Serlio, *Tutte l'opera d'architettura* (1584).

Put not another sin upon my head
By urging me to fury. O, begone!
By heaven, I love thee better than myself,
For I come hither armed against myself.   65
Stay not, begone, live, and hereafter say
A madman's mercy bid thee run away.

PARIS
I do defy thy ⌜commination⌝
And apprehend thee for a felon here.

ROMEO
Wilt thou provoke me? Then have at thee, boy!   70
    ⌜*They draw and fight.*⌝

⌜PAGE⌝
O Lord, they fight! I will go call the watch.
    ⌜*He exits.*⌝

PARIS
O, I am slain! If thou be merciful,
Open the tomb; lay me with Juliet.   ⌜*He dies.*⌝

ROMEO
In faith, I will.—Let me peruse this face.
Mercutio's kinsman, noble County Paris!   75
What said my man when my betossèd soul
Did not attend him as we rode? I think
He told me Paris should have married Juliet.
Said he not so? Or did I dream it so?
Or am I mad, hearing him talk of Juliet,   80
To think it was so?—O, give me thy hand,
One writ with me in sour misfortune's book!
I'll bury thee in a triumphant grave.—
    ⌜*He opens the tomb.*⌝
A grave? O, no. A lantern, slaughtered youth,
For here lies Juliet, and her beauty makes   85
This vault a feasting presence full of light.—
Death, lie thou there, by a dead man interred.
    ⌜*Laying Paris in the tomb.*⌝
How oft when men are at the point of death

90. **light'ning:** sudden lifting of the spirits

94. **ensign:** military flag or banner

97. **sheet:** shroud

98. **more:** greater

100. **his:** i.e., Romeo's

106. **still:** always

110. **set . . . rest:** venture everything (from the card game primero); also, rest here forever

114–15. **seal . . . death:** The legal language that begins with **seal** is carried through in **bargain** (contract) and **engrossing** (monopolizing, buying up in quantity).

116. **conduct:** guide

117. **pilot:** i.e., pilot of a sailing vessel (**bark**) (Romeo here addresses himself.)

Have they been merry, which their keepers call
A light'ning before death! O, how may I   90
Call this a light'ning?—O my love, my wife,
Death, that hath sucked the honey of thy breath,
Hath had no power yet upon thy beauty.
Thou art not conquered. Beauty's ensign yet
Is crimson in thy lips and in thy cheeks,   95
And death's pale flag is not advancèd there.—
Tybalt, liest thou there in thy bloody sheet?
O, what more favor can I do to thee
Than with that hand that cut thy youth in twain
To sunder his that was thine enemy?   100
Forgive me, cousin.—Ah, dear Juliet,
Why art thou yet so fair? Shall I believe
That unsubstantial death is amorous,
And that the lean abhorrèd monster keeps
Thee here in dark to be his paramour?   105
For fear of that I still will stay with thee
And never from this ⌜palace⌝ of dim night
Depart again. Here, here will I remain
With worms that are thy chambermaids. O, here
Will I set up my everlasting rest   110
And shake the yoke of inauspicious stars
From this world-wearied flesh! Eyes, look your last.
Arms, take your last embrace. And, lips, O, you
The doors of breath, seal with a righteous kiss
A dateless bargain to engrossing death.   115
                      ⌜*Kissing Juliet.*⌝
Come, bitter conduct, come, unsavory guide!
Thou desperate pilot, now at once run on
The dashing rocks thy seasick weary bark!
Here's to my love. ⌜*Drinking.*⌝ O true apothecary,
Thy drugs are quick. Thus with a kiss I die.   120
                        ⌜*He dies.*⌝

Enter Friar ⌜*Lawrence*⌝ *with lantern, crow, and spade.*

121. **be my speed:** i.e., help me
140. **ill unthrifty:** evil and unlucky

FRIAR LAWRENCE
　Saint Francis be my speed! How oft tonight
　Have my old feet stumbled at graves!—Who's there?
⌜BALTHASAR⌝
　Here's one, a friend, and one that knows you well.
FRIAR LAWRENCE
　Bliss be upon you. Tell me, good my friend,
　What torch is yond that vainly lends his light   125
　To grubs and eyeless skulls? As I discern,
　It burneth in the Capels' monument.
⌜BALTHASAR⌝
　It doth so, holy sir, and there's my master,
　One that you love.
FRIAR LAWRENCE   Who is it?   130
⌜BALTHASAR⌝   Romeo.
FRIAR LAWRENCE
　How long hath he been there?
⌜BALTHASAR⌝   Full half an hour.
FRIAR LAWRENCE
　Go with me to the vault.
⌜BALTHASAR⌝   I dare not, sir.   135
　My master knows not but I am gone hence,
　And fearfully did menace me with death
　If I did stay to look on his intents.
FRIAR LAWRENCE
　Stay, then. I'll go alone. Fear comes upon me.
　O, much I fear some ill unthrifty thing.   140
⌜BALTHASAR⌝
　As I did sleep under this ⌜yew⌝ tree here,
　I dreamt my master and another fought,
　And that my master slew him.
FRIAR LAWRENCE, ⌜*moving toward the tomb*⌝
                    Romeo!—
　Alack, alack, what blood is this which stains   145
　The stony entrance of this sepulcher?
　What mean these masterless and gory swords

150. **unkind:** (1) unnatural; (2) cruel

151. **lamentable:** accented on the first and third syllables

153. **comfortable:** comfort-bringing

167. **timeless:** (1) untimely, premature; (2) eternal

168. **churl:** selfish one, miser

171. **with a restorative:** i.e., with Romeo's kiss, which should be for her like a restorative medicine

174. **happy:** fortunate

To lie discolored by this place of peace?
Romeo! O, pale! Who else? What, Paris too?
And steeped in blood? Ah, what an unkind hour   150
Is guilty of this lamentable chance!
The lady stirs.

JULIET
O comfortable Friar, where is my lord?
I do remember well where I should be,
And there I am. Where is my Romeo?   155

FRIAR LAWRENCE
I hear some noise.—Lady, come from that nest
Of death, contagion, and unnatural sleep.
A greater power than we can contradict
Hath thwarted our intents. Come, come away.
Thy husband in thy bosom there lies dead,   160
And Paris, too. Come, I'll dispose of thee
Among a sisterhood of holy nuns.
Stay not to question, for the watch is coming.
Come, go, good Juliet. I dare no longer stay.

JULIET
Go, get thee hence, for I will not away.   165
                                        He exits.
What's here? A cup closed in my true love's hand?
Poison, I see, hath been his timeless end.—
O churl, drunk all, and left no friendly drop
To help me after! I will kiss thy lips.
Haply some poison yet doth hang on them,   170
To make me die with a restorative. ⌐*She kisses him.*⌐
Thy lips are warm!

        Enter ⌐*Paris's Page*⌐ *and Watch.*

⌐FIRST⌐ WATCH   Lead, boy. Which way?
JULIET
Yea, noise? Then I'll be brief. O, happy dagger,
This is thy sheath. There rust, and let me die.   175
    ⌐*She takes Romeo's dagger, stabs herself, and dies.*⌐

179. **attach:** arrest
185. **ground:** earth; **woes:** i.e., the corpses
186. **ground:** cause; **woes:** sorrows
187. **circumstance:** details; **descry:** discover
190. **in safety:** i.e., securely
194. **great:** i.e., cause for great
196. **our person:** The Prince uses the royal "we."

⌜PAGE⌝
  This is the place, there where the torch doth burn.
⌜FIRST⌝ WATCH
  The ground is bloody.—Search about the
    churchyard.
  Go, some of you; whoe'er you find, attach.
                              ⌜*Some watchmen exit.*⌝
  Pitiful sight! Here lies the County slain,   180
  And Juliet bleeding, warm, and newly dead,
  Who here hath lain this two days burièd.—
  Go, tell the Prince. Run to the Capulets.
  Raise up the Montagues. Some others search.
                                    ⌜*Others exit.*⌝
  We see the ground whereon these woes do lie,   185
  But the true ground of all these piteous woes
  We cannot without circumstance descry.

      Enter ⌜*Watchmen with*⌝ *Romeo's man* ⌜*Balthasar.*⌝

⌜SECOND⌝ WATCH
  Here's Romeo's man. We found him in the
    churchyard.
⌜FIRST⌝ WATCH
  Hold him in safety till the Prince come hither.   190

      Enter Friar ⌜*Lawrence*⌝ *and another Watchman.*

THIRD WATCH
  Here is a friar that trembles, sighs, and weeps.
  We took this mattock and this spade from him
  As he was coming from this churchyard's side.
⌜FIRST⌝ WATCH
  A great suspicion. Stay the Friar too.

      Enter the Prince ⌜*with Attendants.*⌝

PRINCE
  What misadventure is so early up   195
  That calls our person from our morning rest?

201. **startles:** i.e., sounds startlingly
205. **know:** learn
211. **mista'en:** mistaken (its proper place); **his house:** its sheath
215. **warns:** summons

Enter ⌜Capulet and Lady Capulet.⌝

CAPULET
  What should it be that is so ⌜shrieked⌝ abroad?
LADY CAPULET
  O, the people in the street cry "Romeo,"
  Some "Juliet," and some "Paris," and all run
  With open outcry toward our monument.   200
PRINCE
  What fear is this which startles in ⌜our⌝ ears?
⌜FIRST⌝ WATCH
  Sovereign, here lies the County Paris slain,
  And Romeo dead, and Juliet, dead before,
  Warm and new killed.
PRINCE
  Search, seek, and know how this foul murder   205
    comes.
⌜FIRST⌝ WATCH
  Here is a friar, and ⌜slaughtered⌝ Romeo's man,
  With instruments upon them fit to open
  These dead men's tombs.
CAPULET
  O heavens! O wife, look how our daughter bleeds! 210
  This dagger hath mista'en, for, lo, his house
  Is empty on the back of Montague,
  And it mis-sheathèd in my daughter's bosom.
LADY CAPULET
  O me, this sight of death is as a bell
  That warns my old age to a sepulcher.   215

Enter Montague.

PRINCE
  Come Montague, for thou art early up
  To see thy son and heir now ⌜early⌝ down.
MONTAGUE
  Alas, my liege, my wife is dead tonight.

223. **press:** hurry, thrust yourself forward

224. **outrage:** outcry

226. **spring:** source; **head:** fountainhead, source

230. **let . . . patience:** i.e., let calmness master your misfortunes

231. **parties of suspicion:** i.e., suspicious parties

232. **greatest:** i.e., most suspicious

234. **make:** i.e., provide evidence

235–36. **impeach . . . excused:** i.e., accuse myself of that for which I should be condemned and clear myself of that of which I should be found innocent

238. **date of breath:** lifetime

242. **stol'n:** secret

247. **perforce:** under compulsion

Grief of my son's exile hath stopped her breath.
What further woe conspires against mine age?   220
PRINCE   Look, and thou shalt see.
MONTAGUE, ⌜*seeing Romeo dead*⌝
    O thou untaught! What manners is in this,
    To press before thy father to a grave?
PRINCE
    Seal up the mouth of outrage for awhile,
    Till we can clear these ambiguities   225
    And know their spring, their head, their true
        descent,
    And then will I be general of your woes
    And lead you even to death. Meantime forbear,
    And let mischance be slave to patience.—   230
    Bring forth the parties of suspicion.
FRIAR LAWRENCE
    I am the greatest, able to do least,
    Yet most suspected, as the time and place
    Doth make against me, of this direful murder.
    And here I stand, both to impeach and purge   235
    Myself condemnèd and myself excused.
PRINCE
    Then say at once what thou dost know in this.
FRIAR LAWRENCE
    I will be brief, for my short date of breath
    Is not so long as is a tedious tale.
    Romeo, there dead, was husband to that Juliet,   240
    And she, there dead, ⌜that⌝ Romeo's faithful wife.
    I married them, and their stol'n marriage day
    Was Tybalt's doomsday, whose untimely death
    Banished the new-made bridegroom from this city,
    For whom, and not for Tybalt, Juliet pined.   245
    You, to remove that siege of grief from her,
    Betrothed and would have married her perforce
    To County Paris. Then comes she to me,
    And with wild looks bid me devise some mean

252. **art:** i.e., skill in medicine
256. **as this:** i.e., this
262. **prefixèd:** predetermined
264. **closely:** secretly
272. **desperate:** in despair
275. **is privy:** knows the secret
277. **some . . . time:** i.e., an hour or so before its time (to end)
279. **still:** always
282. **in post:** in haste

To rid her from this second marriage, 250
Or in my cell there would she kill herself.
Then gave I her (so tutored by my art)
A sleeping potion, which so took effect
As I intended, for it wrought on her
The form of death. Meantime I writ to Romeo 255
That he should hither come as this dire night
To help to take her from her borrowed grave,
Being the time the potion's force should cease.
But he which bore my letter, Friar John,
Was stayed by accident, and yesternight 260
Returned my letter back. Then all alone
At the prefixèd hour of her waking
Came I to take her from her kindred's vault,
Meaning to keep her closely at my cell
Till I conveniently could send to Romeo. 265
But when I came, some minute ere the time
Of her awakening, here untimely lay
The noble Paris and true Romeo dead.
She wakes, and I entreated her come forth
And bear this work of heaven with patience. 270
But then a noise did scare me from the tomb,
And she, too desperate, would not go with me
But, as it seems, did violence on herself.
All this I know, and to the marriage
Her nurse is privy. And if aught in this 275
Miscarried by my fault, let my old life
Be sacrificed some hour before his time
Unto the rigor of severest law.

PRINCE
We still have known thee for a holy man.—
Where's Romeo's man? What can he say to this? 280

BALTHASAR
I brought my master news of Juliet's death,
And then in post he came from Mantua
To this same place, to this same monument.

284. **he . . . father:** i.e., he instructed me to give his father early this morning

285. **going:** i.e., as he was going

288. **that raised:** i.e., who alerted

290. **what made your master:** i.e., what was your master doing

299. **therewithal:** i.e., with the poison

303. **your joys:** i.e., your children

304. **winking at:** closing my eyes to

307. **jointure:** the present given the bride by the groom's family

310. **ray:** i.e., array, dress (**Ray** is the reading of the Second Quarto; the alternative and more familiar reading, "raise," is found in the Fourth Quarto and the Folio. But Montague is evidently promising to gold-plate the figure of Juliet that would customarily lie on top of her tomb or sarcophagus. Compare the "gilded monuments" of Shakespeare's Sonnet 55.)

311. **whiles:** as long as

312. **figure:** statue; **at . . . set:** be valued as greatly

This letter he early bid me give his father
And threatened me with death, going in the vault,   285
If I departed not and left him there.
PRINCE
Give me the letter. I will look on it.—
       ⌜*He takes Romeo's letter.*⌝
Where is the County's page, that raised the
  watch?—
Sirrah, what made your master in this place?   290
PAGE
He came with flowers to strew his lady's grave
And bid me stand aloof, and so I did.
Anon comes one with light to ope the tomb,
And by and by my master drew on him,
And then I ran away to call the watch.   295
PRINCE
This letter doth make good the Friar's words,
Their course of love, the tidings of her death;
And here he writes that he did buy a poison
Of a poor 'pothecary, and therewithal
Came to this vault to die and lie with Juliet.   300
Where be these enemies?—Capulet, Montague,
See what a scourge is laid upon your hate,
That heaven finds means to kill your joys with love,
And I, for winking at your discords too,
Have lost a brace of kinsmen. All are punished.   305
CAPULET
O brother Montague, give me thy hand.
This is my daughter's jointure, for no more
Can I demand.
MONTAGUE   But I can give thee more,
For I will ray her statue in pure gold,   310
That whiles Verona by that name is known,
There shall no figure at such rate be set
As that of true and faithful Juliet.

314. **Romeo's:** i.e., Romeo's statue

CAPULET
  As rich shall Romeo's by his lady's lie,
  Poor sacrifices of our enmity.   315
PRINCE
  A glooming peace this morning with it brings.
  The sun for sorrow will not show his head.
  Go hence to have more talk of these sad things.
  Some shall be pardoned, and some punishèd.
  For never was a story of more woe   320
  Than this of Juliet and her Romeo.
                              ⌜*All exit.*⌝

Textual Notes

The reading of the present text appears to the left of the square bracket. The earliest sources of readings not in **Q2**, the quarto of 1599 (upon which this edition is based, except for 1.2.55– 1.3.37, which are based on the 1597 quarto), are indicated as follows: **Q1** is the quarto of 1597; **Q3** is that of 1609; **Q4** is that of 1622; and **F** is the Shakespeare First Folio of 1623, in which *Romeo and Juliet* is a slightly edited reprint of Q3. **Ed.** is an earlier editor of Shakespeare, from the editor of the Second Folio of 1632 to the present. No sources are given for emendations of punctuation or for correction of obvious typographical errors, such as turned letters that produce no known word. **SD** means stage direction; **SP** means speech prefix; **uncorr.** means the uncorrected, or first state in Q2; **corr.** means the corrected, or second state in Q2; ~ refers to a word already quoted; ‸ indicates the omission of a punctuation mark.

1.1. 28. in] Q1; *omit* Q2 33. SD *Enter . . . Servingman.*] this ed.; *Enter two other seruing men.* Q2 74. SP CITIZENS] Ed.; *Offi.* Q2 77. SP LADY CAPULET] Ed.; *Wife.* Q2 78. SD *2 lines later in* Q2 82. SP LADY MONTAGUE] Ed.; M. *Wife.* 2. Q2 94. Verona's] *Neronas* Q2 118. SP LADY MONTAGUE] Ed.; *Wife* Q2 122. drove] Q3 (draue); driue Q2 123. sycamore] Syramour Q2 150. his] Q3; is Q2 182. create] Q1; created Q2 184. well- seeming] Q4; welseeing Q2 223. rich in beauty] ~, ~~ Q2 226. makes] Q4; make Q2

1.2. 0. SD *a Servingman*] Ed.; *the Clowne* Q2 21. guest‸] ~: Q2 23. welcome,] ~‸ Q2 32. on] Q2 (one) 38. SD *Capulet . . . exit.*] Ed.; *Exit.* Q2 39–40. written here] ~.~Q2 48. One] Q2 (On) 71. *Vitruvio*] Ed.; Vtruuio Q1, Q2 75. and] Q1; *omit* Q2 84. thee] Q1; you Q2

1.3. 0. SD *Lady Capulet*] Ed.; *Capulets wife* Q1, Q2 1, 8, 13, 17. SP LADY CAPULET] Ed.; *Wife.* Q1, Q2 1. daughter?] ~ ‸

245

Q1 12. an] Q2; a Q1 19. shall] Q1; stal Q2 34. the] Q2; *omit*
Q1 54, 68, 75, 83, 102. SP LADY CAPULET] Ed.; *Old La.* Q2 70.
disposition] Ed.; dispositions Q2 71, 72. honor] Q1; houre
Q2 77. mothers. . . . count‸] ‿ ‸ . . . ‿. Q2 101. bigger.] ‿ ‸
Q2 105. it] Q1; *omit* Q2 105. SD *Servingman*] F; *Seruing.*
Q2 111. SP LADY CAPULET] Ed.; *Mo.* Q2

1.4 7–8. Q1; *omit* Q2 23. SP MERCUTIO] Q4; *Horatio* Q2
39. done] Q1; dum Q2 42. your] F; you Q2 47. lights;
. . . light] Ed.; ‿ ‸ . . . lights Q2 48. judgment] indgement Q2
49. five 2] Ed.; fine Q2 62. atomi] Q1; ottamie Q2 71.
maid] Q1; man Q2 76. love;] ‿. Q2 79. on] Q2 (one) 81.
breaths] Q1 (breathes); breath Q2 86. he dreams] *stet* Q2
95. elflocks] Q1; Elklocks Q2 118. forfeit] fofreit Q2 120.
sail] Q1; sute Q2

1.5. 0. SD *napkins*] F; *Napkins.* | *Enter* Romeo. Q2 1, 7, 13.
SP FIRST SERVINGMAN] Ed.; *Ser.* Q2 4. SP SECOND SERVING-
MAN] Ed.; 1. Q2 12. SP THIRD SERVINGMAN] Ed.; 2. Q2 15. SP
THIRD SERVINGMAN] Ed.; 3. Q2 17. SD *They . . . aside.*] this
ed.; *Exeunt.* Q2 18, 40, 46. SP CAPULET] Q1; 1. *Capu.* Q2 19. a
bout] Ed.; about Q2 21. mistresses] mistesses Q2 29. gentlemen.] ‿ ‸ Q2 39, 44. SP CAPULET'S COUSIN] Ed.; 2 *Capu.*
Q2 41. Lucentio] Q1; Lucientio Q2 95. you.] ‿ ‸ Q2 106.
pilgrims, ready] Q1; pilgrims did readie Q2 156. this?] this. Q2
uncorr. (tis.); tis‸ Q2 *corr.*

2. Chor. 4. matched] Q3; match Q2

2.1 8. SP MERCUTIO] Q1; *omit* Q2 9. Romeo] Q1; *Mer.*
Romeo Q2 11. one] Q2 (on) 12. pronounce] Q1; prouaunt
Q2 13. "dove"] Q1; day Q2 15. heir] Q1; her Q2 16. Abra-
ham‸ Cupid,] ‿:‿ ‸ Q2 trim] Q1; true Q2 36. SP MERCU-
TIO] Q3; *Mar.* Q2 41. open-arse] Ed.; open, or Q2 46. SD
They exit.] Q4; *Exit.* Q2

2.2. 16. do] Q1; to Q2 44. nor any other part] Q1; *omit*
Q2 45. Belonging . . . name] Ed.; O be some other name |
Belonging to a man Q2 46. name? That] ‿ ‸ ‿ Q2 48. were]
Q3; wene Q2 70. kinsmen] kismen Q2 88. washed] Q1;
washeth Q2 97. false. . . . perjuries,]‿ ‸ . . . ‿.Q2 104. hav-
ior] Q1; behauior Q2 106. more] Q1; *omit* Q2 115. circled]

Q1; circle Q2   155. lord] Q1; L. Q2   159–60. Madam . . .
come] Ed.; (by and by I come) Madam. Q2   173. mine]
Q1; *omit* Q2   179. dear] Q4; Neece Q2   202. SP ROMEO] Q1;
Iu. Q2   203. Would] Q4; *Ro.* Would Q2   203. rest.] Q1; rest |
The grey eyde morne smiles on the frowning night, | Checkring
the Easterne Clouds with streaks of light, | And darknesse
fleckted like a drunkard reeles, | From forth daies pathway,
made by *Tytans* wheeles. Q2

2.3.   1 *and throughout until* 5.2. SP FRIAR LAWRENCE] Ed.; *Fri.*
Q2   2. Check'ring] Q2 2.2.203 (above); Checking Q2 2.3.2   4.
fiery] Q1; burning Q2   13. many ͵ virtues] ~, ~ Q2   55.
wounded. Both ͵] ~ ͵ ~, Q2   71. Young] yonng Q2   91. now ͵]
~. Q2

2.4.   0. SD *Enter*] *Bnter* Q2   7. kinsman] kisman Q2   19. SP
BENVOLIO] Q1; *Ro.* Q2   30. phantasimes] Ed.; phantacies Q2
34–35. "pardon-me" 's] Q1; pardons mees Q2   41. Petrarch]
Petrach Q2   103. SD *one-half line later in* Q2   165. quivers.] ~,
Q2   212. Ah,] A ͵ Q2   212. dog's name. *R*] Q3; dog, name *R.*
Q2   213. the—No] ~ ͵ ~ Q2   219. SD *They exit.*] Q1 *(Ex.
omnes.); Exit.* Q2

2.5   7. Love] F; loue Q2   11. three] Q3; there Q2   15. And]
Q4; *M.* And Q2   41. he.] ~ ͵ Q2   59. and] Q2 (An)

2.6.   27. music's] Q4; musicke Q2

3.1.   2. are] Q1; *omit* Q2   70. thou] thon Q2   91. SD *Romeo
. . . Mercutio.*] this ed.; *omit* Q2; *Tibalt vnder Romeos arme
thrusts Mercutio, in and flyes.* Q1   92. SP PETRUCHIO] Ed.; *omit*
Q2, *which sets this speech as a* SD   113. soundly, too. Your] Ed.;
soundly ͵ to ͵ your Q2   113. SD *All . . . exit.*] Ed.; *Exit.* Q2
122. gallant] gallanr Q2   127. Alive] Q1; He gan Q2   129.
fire-eyed] Q1; fier and Q2   144, 147. SP CITIZEN] Ed.; *Citti. (Citi.
147)* Q2   145. murderer] mutherer Q2   153, 156. kinsman]
kisman Q2   154, 185. SP LADY CAPULET] Ed.; *Capu. Wi.(Ca. Wi.
185)* Q2   163. displeasure.] ~ ͵ Q2   175. agile] Q1; aged
Q2   185. kinsman] kisman Q2   193. SP MONTAGUE] Q4;
Capu. Q2   202. I] Q1; It Q2   207. SD *They . . . body.*] this ed.;
Exit. Q2

3.2.   1. SP JULIET] Q1; *omit* Q2   9. By] Q4; And by Q2   33.

SD *one-half line later in* Q2   48. it?] ~ₐ Q2   53. death-darting]
death arting Q2   55. shut] Ed.; shot Q2   57. Briefₐ soundsₐ]
~, ~, Q2   57. determine my] Q2 *stet;* determine of my F   66.
one] Q2 (on)   78. SP NURSE] Q1; *omit* Q2   79. SP JULIET] Q1;
Nur. Q2   80. Did] Ed.; *Iu.* Did Q2   82. Dove-feathered] Ed.;
Rauenous doue-featherd Q2   85. damnèd] Q4; dimme Q2
157. SD *They exit.*] Q1; *Exit.* Q2

3.3.   0. SD *Enter . . . Lawrence.*] Ed.; *Enter Frier and* Romeo.
Q2   20. is banished] Q3; is blanisht Q2   41–46. sin . . . Hadst]
Ed.; sin. | This may flyes do, when I from this must flie, | And
sayest thou yet, that exile is not death? | But *Romeo* may not, he
is banished. | Flies may do this, but I from this must flie: | They
are freemen, but I am banished. | Hadst Q2   53. absolver] Q2
(obsoluer)   55. Thou] Q1; Then Q2   64. madmen] Q1; mad
man Q2   71. mightst] Q1; mightest Q2   74. SD *Knock within.*]
Ed.; *Enter Nurse, and knocke.* Q2   77. SD *Knock.*] Q4; *They
knocke.* Q2   80. SD *Knock.*] F; *Slud knock.* Q2   85. SP NURSE,
within] Ed.; *Enter Nurse.* | *Nur.* Q2   120. denote] Q1; deuote
Q2   127. lives] Ed.; lies Q2   146–47. dead: . . . happy.]
~ . . . . ~, Q2   153. misbehaved] Q1; mishaued Q2   154. pouts
upon] Q4; puts vp Q2   175. comfort] eomfort Q2   179. dis-
guised] Q3; disguise Q2

3.4.   11. SP LADY CAPULET] Ed.; *La.* Q2   14. be] Q1; me
Q2   26. We'llₐ] Q1; Well, Q2

3.5.   13. exhaled] Ed.; exhale Q2   19. the] the the Q2   31.
changed] Ed.; change Q2   36. SD *Enter Nurse.*] Ed.; *Enter
Madame and Nurse.* Q2   54. SP JULIET] Q1; *Ro.* Q2   55. thee,
nowₐ] ~ₐ~, Q2   64. SD *Enter Lady Capulet.*] Ed.; *Enter
Mother.* Q2   65, 69, 71, 78, 82, 85, 89, 92, 144, 163. SP LADY
CAPULET] Ed.; *La.* Q2   87. pardon] Q3; padon Q2   87. him] Q4;
omit Q2   99. him—dead—] ~. ~ₐ Q2   108, 214. SP LADY
CAPULET] Ed.; *Mo.* Q2   112, 117, 129. SP LADY CAPULET] Ed.; *M.*
Q2   135. show'ring? . . . bodyₐ] ~ₐ . . . ~? Q2   136. counter-
feitsₐ] ~. Q2   144. gives] Q3; giue Q2   156. proud? . . . you,]
~ₐ . . . ~? Q2   166, 178, 183, 187. SP CAPULET] Ed.; *Fa.* Q2   179.
Prudence, smatterₐ]~ₐ~, Q2   181. SP CAPULET O] Q1; Father O
Q2   182. SP NURSE] Q4; *omit* Q2   186. SP LADY CAPULET]

Ed.; *Wi.* Q2   192. ligned] Ed.; liand Q2   246. absolved] Q2
(obsolu'd)

4.1.   73. slay] Q1; stay Q2   79. off] Q2 (of)   84. chapless]
Q1; chapels Q2   86. shroud] Q4; *omit* Q2   100. breath] Q1;
breast Q2   101. fade‸] ~: Q2   102. paly] Q4; many Q2   102.
fall ‸] ~: Q2   112. In] Q3; Is Q2 . 112–13. bier ǀ Thou] Ed.;
Beere, ǀ Be borne to buriall in thy kindreds graue: ǀ Thou
Q2   113. shalt] Q3; shall Q2   117. and] Q2 (an)   118. waking]
Q3; walking Q2   123. fear] Q2 *uncorr.* (feare); fea re Q2
corr.   129. SD *They . . . directions.*] this ed.; *Exit.* Q2

4.2.   3, 6. SP SERVINGMAN] Ed.; *Ser.* Q2   14. self-willed
harlotry] Q3; selfewield harlottry Q2 *uncorr.;* selfewieldhar
lottry Q2 *corr.*   27. becomèd] Q4; becomd Q2   37, 39. SP LADY
CAPULET] Ed.; *Mo.* Q2   38, 41. SP CAPULET] Ed.; *Fa.* Q2   38. SD
Juliet . . . exit.] Q1; *Exeunt.* Q2   49. SD *They exit.*] Q1; *Exit.* Q2

4.3.   5. SD *Lady Capulet*] Ed.; *Mother* Q2   6, 13. SP LADY
CAPULET] Ed.; *Mo.* Q2   14. SD *Lady . . . exit.*] Ed.; *Exeunt.*
Q2   50. wake] Q4; walke Q2   60. SD *She . . . curtains.*] this
ed.; *omit* Q2; *She fals vpon her bed within the Curtaines.* Q1

4.4.   0. SD *Lady Capulet*] Ed.; *Lady of the house* Q2   1, 12. SP
LADY CAPULET] Ed.; *La.* Q2   13. SD *Lady Capulet*] Ed.; *Lady*
Q2   14. SD *one-half line earlier in* Q2   17. SP FIRST SERVING-
MAN] Ed.; *Fel.* Q2   18. haste.] ~ ‸ Q2   21. SP SECOND SERVING-
MAN] Ed.; *Fel.* Q2   24. Thou] Q1; Twou Q2   25. faith] Q4; father
Q2   26. SD *Play music.*] *1 line earlier in* Q2

4.5.   20, 22, 24, 29, 36, 49. SP LADY CAPULET] Ed.; *Mo.* (once
M.) Q2   26. SD *Capulet*] Ed.; *Father* Q2   27, 30, 37, 40, 65, 90.
SP CAPULET] Ed.; *Fa.* (once *Fat.*) Q2   43. deflowerèd] Ed.;
deflowred Q2   46. all.] ~ ‸ Q2   47. long] Q1; loue Q2   57.
behold] Q3; bedold Q2   71. cure] Ed.; care Q2   72. confu-
sions.] ~ ‸ Q2   88. fond] Ed.; some Q2   101. SD *All . . . exit.*]
Ed.; *Fxeunt manet.* Q2   102. SP FIRST MUSICIAN] Ed.; *Musi.*
Q2   105. SP FIRST MUSICIAN] Ed.; *Fid.* Q2   105. by] Q1; my
Q2   105. SD *Nurse exits.*] Q1 (*1 line earlier*); *Exit omnes.*
Q2   105. SD *Peter*] Q4; *Will Kemp* Q2   109. SP FIRST MUSICIAN]
Ed.; *Fidler.* Q2   113. SP FIRST MUSICIAN] Ed.; *Minstrels.* Q2
116, 118, 126, 137. SP FIRST MUSICIAN] Ed.; *Minst.* Q2   121. SP

FIRST MUSICIAN] Ed.; *Minstrel.* Q2   127, 140. SP SECOND MUSI-
CIAN] Ed.; 2. *M.* Q2   129. SP PETER] Q4; *omit* Q2   129. wit. I]
Q4; wit. I *Peter* I Q2   133. *And . . . oppress*] Q1; *omit* Q2   143.
SP THIRD MUSICIAN] Ed.; 3. *M.* Q2   149. SP FIRST MUSICIAN] Ed.;
Min. Q2   150. SP SECOND MUSICIAN] Ed.; *M.* 2. Q2   151. SD
They exit.] Q1; *Exit.* Q2

5.1.   3. lord] Q1; L. Q2   12. SD *Balthasar in riding boots*] this
ed.; *Balthasar his man booted* Q1; *omit* Q2   16. Juliet] Q1; Lady
Juliet Q2   18, 28, 34. SP BALTHASAR] Q1; *Man.* Q2   25. e'en]
Q2 (in)   25. defy] Q1; denie Q2   36. SD *Exit., 2 lines earlier in*
Q2   62. SP ROMEO] *Kom.* Q2   70, 79, 81. SP APOTHECARY] Q1;
Poti. Q2   80. pay] Q1; pray Q2   91. SD *He exits.*] Ed.; *Exeunt.*
Q2

5.2.   0. SD Q2 *adds "to Frier* Lawrence"   1, 5, 14. SP FRIAR
JOHN] Ed.; *Ioh.* (twice *Iohn.*) Q2   2, 13, 17. SP FRIAR LAW-
RENCE] Ed.; *Law.* Q2

5.3.   3, 141. yew] Q1 (Ew, 3); young Q2   17. SD *Page
whistles.*] Ed.; *Whistle Boy.* Q2   21. SD *Balthasar*] Q1; *Peter*
Q2   25. light.] ~ ˏ Q2   40, 43. SP BALTHASAR] Q1 *(Balt.); Peter*
Q2   41. friendship] Q3; friendshid Q2   45. SD *beginning to
force open the tomb*] Ed.; *Romeo opens the tombe.* Q1; *omit*
Q2   68. commination] Ed.; commiration Q2   70. SD *They
draw and fight.*] *They fight.* Q1; *omit* Q2   71. SP PAGE] Ed.; *Boy*
Q1; *omit* Q2, *which sets this speech as a stage direction*   102.
Shall] Ed.; I will beleeue I Shall Q2   107. palace] Q3; pallat
Q2   107. nightˏ] ~. Q2   108. Depart again. Here] Q4; Depart
againe, come lye thou in my arme, I Heer's to thy health, where
ere thou tumblest in. I O true Appothecarie! I Thy drugs are
quicke. Thus with a kisse I die. I Depart againe, here Q2   120.
SD *Enter*] Q3; *Entrer* Q2   121 *and throughout* SP FRIAR
LAWRENCE] Ed.; *Frier.* Q2   123, 128, 131, 133, 135, 141. SP
BALTHASAR] Q4; *Man.* Q2   156. noise.] ~ ˏ Q2   165. SD *He
exits.*] *1 line earlier in* Q2   172. SD *Paris' Page*] Ed.; *Boy*
Q2   173, 177, 202, 207. SP FIRST WATCH] Ed.; *Watch* Q2   176.
SP PAGE] Ed.; *Watch boy* Q2   188. SP SECOND] Ed.; *omit*
Q2   190, 194. SP FIRST] Ed.; *Chief.* Q2   194. too.] too too.
Q2   196. SD *Capulet and Lady Capulet*] Ed.; *Capels* Q2   197.
shrieked] Ed.; shrike Q2   198, 214. SP LADY CAPULET] Ed.;

Wife. Q2   201. our] Ed.; your Q2   207. slaughtered] Q3;
Slaughter Q2   209. SD tombs.] Tombes. *Enter Capulet and his
wife.* Q2   213. mis-sheathèd] missheathd Q2   217. early] Q1;
earling Q2   235. impeach] Q2 *uncorr.;* i peach Q2 *corr.*   241.
that] Q1; thats Q2   283. place, . . . monument.] ~. . . . ~ ‿
Q2   291. SP PAGE] F; *Boy* Q2   302. hate,]~? Q2

Romeo and Juliet:
A Modern Perspective

Gail Kern Paster

Does *Romeo and Juliet* need an introduction? Of all Shakespeare's plays, it has been the most continuously popular since its first performance in the mid-1590s. It would seem, then, the most direct of Shakespeare's plays in its emotional impact. What could be easier to understand and what could be more moving than the story of two adolescents finding in their sudden love for each other a reason to defy their families' mutual hatred by marrying secretly? The tragic outcome of their blameless love (their "misadventured piteous over-throws") seems equally easy to understand: it results first from Tybalt's hotheaded refusal to obey the Prince's command and second from accidents of timing beyond any human ability to foresee or control. Simple in its story line, clear in its affirmation of the power of love over hate, *Romeo and Juliet* seems to provide both a timeless theme and universal appeal. Its immediacy stands in welcome contrast to the distance, even es-trangement, evoked by other Shakespeare plays. No wonder it is often the first Shakespeare play taught in schools—on the grounds of its obvious relevance to the emotional and social concerns of young people.

Recent work by social historians on the history of private life in Western European culture, however, offers a complicating perspective on the timelessness of *Romeo and Juliet*. At the core of the play's evident accessibility is the importance and privilege modern Western culture grants to desire, regarding it as deeply expressive of individual identity and central to the

253

personal fulfillment of women no less than men. But, as these historians have argued, such conceptions of desire reflect cultural changes in human consciousness—in ways of imagining and articulating the nature of desire.[1] In England until the late sixteenth century, individual identity had been imagined not so much as the result of autonomous, personal growth in consciousness but rather as a function of social station, an individual's place in a network of social and kinship structures. Furthermore, traditional culture distinguished sharply between the nature of identity for men and women. A woman's identity was conceived almost exclusively in relation to male authority and marital status. She was less an autonomous, desiring self than any male was; she was a daughter, wife, or widow expected to be chaste, silent, and, above all, obedient. It is a profound and necessary act of historical imagination, then, to recognize innovation in the moment when Juliet impatiently invokes the coming of night and the husband she has disobediently married: "Come, gentle night; come, loving black-browed night, / Give me my Romeo" (3.2.21–23).

Recognizing that the nature of desire and identity is subject to historical change and cultural innovation can provide the basis for rereading *Romeo and Juliet*. Instead of an uncomplicated, if lyrically beautiful, contest between young love and "ancient grudge," the play becomes a narrative that expresses an historical conflict between old forms of identity and new modes of desire, between authority and freedom, between parental will and romantic individualism. Furthermore, though the Chorus initially sets the lovers *as a pair* against the background of familial hatred, the reader attentive to social detail will be struck instead by Shakespeare's care in distinguishing between the circumstances of male and female lovers: "she as much in love, *her means much less* / To meet her new belovèd anywhere" (2. Chorus.

11-12). The story of "Juliet and her Romeo" may be a single narrative, but its clear internal division is drawn along the traditionally unequal lines of gender.

Because of such traditional notions of identity and gender, Elizabethan theatergoers might have recognized a paradox in the play's lyrical celebration of the beauty of awakened sexual desire in the adolescent boy and girl. By causing us to identify with Romeo and Juliet's desire for one another, the play affirms their love even while presenting it as a problem in social management. This is true not because Romeo and Juliet fall in love with forbidden or otherwise unavailable sexual partners; such is the usual state of affairs at the beginning of Shakespearean comedy, but those comedies end happily. Rather Romeo and Juliet's love is a social problem, unresolvable except by their deaths, because they dare to *marry* secretly in an age when legal, consummated marriage was irreversible. Secret marriage is the narrative device by which Shakespeare brings into conflict the new privilege claimed by individual desire and the traditional authority granted fathers to arrange their daughters' marriages. Secret marriage is the testing ground, in other words, of the new kind of importance being claimed by individual desire. Shakespeare's representation of the narrative outcome of this desire as tragic—here, as later in the secret marriage that opens *Othello*—may suggest something of Elizabethan society's anxiety about the social cost of romantic individualism.

The conflict between traditional authority and individual desire also provides the framework for Shakespeare's presentation of the Capulet-Montague feud. The feud, like the lovers' secret marriage, is another problem in social management, another form of socially problematic desire. We are never told what the families are fighting about or fighting for; in this sense the feud is both causeless and goal-less. The Chorus's first words insist not on the differences between the two families but on their similarity: they are two households "both alike in dignity." Later, after Prince Escalus has broken up the street brawl, they are "In penalty alike" (1.2.2). Ironically, then, they are not fighting over differences. Rather it is Shakespeare's careful insistence on the lack of difference between Montague and Capulet that provides a key to understanding the underlying social dynamic of the feud. Just as desire brings Romeo and Juliet together as lovers, desire in another form brings the Montague and Capulet males out on the street as fighters. The feud perpetuates a close bond of rivalry between these men that even the Prince's threat of punishment cannot sever: "Montague is *bound* as well as I," Capulet tells Paris (1.2.1). Indeed, the feud seems necessary to the structure of male-male relations in Verona. Feuding reinforces male identity—loyalty to one's male ancestors—at the same time that it clarifies the social structure: servants fight with servants, young noblemen with young noblemen, old men with old men.[2]

That the feud constitutes a relation of desire between Montague and Capulet is clear from the opening, when the servants Gregory and Sampson use bawdy innuendo to draw a causal link between their virility and their eagerness to fight Montagues: "A dog of that house shall move me to stand," i.e., to be sexually erect (1.1.12). The Montagues seem essential to Sampson's masculinity since, by besting Montague men, he can lay claim to Montague women as symbols of conquest. (This, of course, would be a reductive way of describing what Romeo does in secretly marrying a Capulet daughter.) The feud not only establishes a structure of relations between men based on competition and sexual aggression, but it seems to involve a particularly debased attitude toward women. No matter how comic the wordplay of the Capulet servants may be, we should not forget that the sexual triangle they imagine is based on fantasized rape: "I will push Montague's men from the wall and thrust his maids to the wall" (1.1.18–19). Gregory and Sampson are not interested in the "heads" of the Montague maidens, which might imply awareness of them as individuals. They are interested only in their "maidenheads." Their coarse view of woman as generic sexual object is reiterated in a wittier vein by Mercutio, who understands Romeo's experience of awakened desire only as a question of the sexual availability of his mistress: "O Romeo, that she were, O, that she were / An open-arse, thou a pop'rin pear" (2.1.40–41).

Feuding, then, is the form that male bonding takes in Verona, a bonding which seems linked to the derogation of woman. But Romeo, from the very opening of the play, is distanced both physically and emotionally from the feud, not appearing until the combatants and his parents are leaving the stage. His reaction to Benvolio's news of the fight seems to indicate that he is aware of the mechanisms of desire that are present in the feud: "Here's much to do with hate, but more with love" (1.1.180). But it also underscores his sense of alienation: "This love feel I, that feel no love in this" (187). He is alienated not only from the feud itself, one feels, but more importantly from the idea of sexuality that underlies it. Romeo subscribes to a different, indeed a competing view of woman—the idealizing view of the Petrarchan lover. In his melancholy, his desire for solitude, and his paradox-strewn language, Romeo identifies himself with the style of feeling and address that Renaissance culture named after the fourteenth-century Italian poet Francesco Petrarca or Petrarch, most famous for his sonnets to Laura. By identifying his beloved as perfect and perfectly chaste, the Petrarchan lover opposes the indiscriminate erotic appetite of a Gregory or

Sampson. He uses the frustrating experience of intense, unfulfilled, and usually unrequited passion to refine his modes of feeling and to enlarge his experience of self.

It is not coincidental, then, that Shakespeare uses the language and self-involved behaviors of the Petrarchan lover to dramatize Romeo's experience of love. For Romeo as for Petrarch, love is the formation of an individualistic identity at odds with other kinds of identity: "I have lost myself. I am not here. / This is not Romeo. He's some other where" (1.1.205–6). Petrarchan desire for solitude explains Romeo's absence from the opening clash and his lack of interest in the activities of his gang of friends, whom he accompanies only reluctantly to the Capulet feast: "I'll be a candle holder and look on" (1.4.38). His physical isolation from his parents—with whom he exchanges no words in the course of the play—further suggests his shift from traditional, clan identity to the romantic individualism prefigured by Petrarch.

Shakespeare's comic irony is that such enlargement of self is itself a mark of conventionality, since Petrarchism in European literature was by the late sixteenth century very widespread. A more cutting irony is that the Petrarchan lover and his sensual opponent (Sampson or Gregory) have more in common than is first apparent. The Petrarchan lover, in emphasizing the often paralyzing intensity of his passion, is less interested in praising the remote mistress who inspires such devotion than he is in displaying his own poetic virtuosity and his capacity for self-denial. Such a love—like Romeo's for Rosaline—is founded upon frustration and requires rejection. The lover is interested in affirming the uniqueness of his beloved only in theory. On closer look, she too becomes a generic object and he more interested in self-display. Thus the play's two languages of heterosexual desire— Petrarchan praise and anti-Petrarchan debasement—

appear as opposite ends of a single continuum, as complementary discourses of woman, high and low. Even when Paris and old Capulet, discussing Juliet as prospective bride, vary the discourse to include a conception of woman as wife and mother, she remains an object of verbal and actual exchange.

In lyric poetry, the Petrarchan mistress remains a function of language alone, unheard, seen only as a collection of ideal parts, a center whose very absence promotes desire. Drama is a material medium, however. In drama, the Petrarchan mistress takes on embodiment and finds an answering voice, like Juliet's gently noting her sonneteer-pilgrim's conventionality: "You kiss by th' book" (1.5.122). In drama, the mistress may come surrounded by relatives and an inconveniently insistent social milieu. As was noted above, Shakespeare distinguishes sharply between the social circumstances of adolescent males and females. Thus one consequence of setting the play's domestic action solely within the Capulet household is to set Juliet, the "hopeful lady" of Capulet's "earth" (1.2.15), firmly into a familial context which, thanks to the Nurse's fondness for recollection and anecdote, is rich in domestic detail. Juliet's intense focus upon Romeo's surname—"What's Montague? . . . O, be some other name" (2.2.43, 45)—is a projection onto her lover of her own conflicted sense of tribal loyalty. Unlike Romeo, whose deepest emotional ties are to his gang of friends, and unlike the more mobile daughters of Shakespearean comedy who often come in pairs, Juliet lives isolated and confined, emotionally as well as physically, by her status as daughter. Her own passage into sexual maturity comes first by way of parental invitation to "think of marriage now" (1.3.75). Her father invites Paris, the man who wishes to marry Juliet, to attend a banquet and feast his eyes on female beauty: "Hear all, all see, / And like her most whose merit most shall be" (1.2.30–31). Juliet, in contrast, is invited to look only where her parents tell her:

> I'll look to like, if looking liking move.
> But no more deep will I endart mine eye
> Than your consent gives strength to make it fly.
> (1.3.103–5)

The logic of Juliet's almost instant disobedience in looking at, and liking, Romeo (rather than Paris) can be understood as the ironic fulfillment of the fears in traditional patriarchal culture about the uncontrollability of female desire, the alleged tendency of the female gaze to wander. Petrarchism managed the vexed question of female desire largely by wishing it out of existence, describing the mistress as one who, like the invisible Rosaline of this play, "will not stay the siege of loving terms, / Nor bide th' encounter of assailing eyes" (1.1.220–21). Once Romeo, in the Capulet garden, overhears Juliet's expression of desire, however, Juliet abandons the conventional denial of desire—"Fain would I dwell on form; fain, fain deny / What I have spoke. But farewell compliment" (2.2.93–94). She rejects the "strength" implied by parental sanction and the protection afforded by the Petrarchan celebration of chastity for a risk-taking experiment in desire that Shakespeare affirms by the beauty of the lovers' language in their four scenes together. Juliet herself asks Romeo the serious questions that Elizabethan society wanted only fathers to ask. She challenges social prescriptions, designed to contain erotic desire in marriage, by taking responsibility for her own marriage:

> If that thy bent of love be honorable,
> Thy purpose marriage, send me word tomorrow,
> By one that I'll procure to come to thee,

Where and what time thou wilt perform the rite,
And all my fortunes at thy foot I'll lay
And follow thee my lord throughout the world.
(2.2.150–55)

The irony in her pledge—an irony perhaps most
obvious to a modern, sexually egalitarian audience—is
that Romeo here is following Juliet on an uncharted
narrative path to sexual fulfillment in unsanctioned
marriage. Allowing her husband access to a bedcham-
ber in her father's house, Juliet leads him into a sexual
territory beyond the reach of dramatic representation.
Breaking through the narrow oppositions of the play's
two discourses of woman—as either anonymous sexual
object (for Sampson and Gregory) or beloved woman
exalted beyond knowing or possessing (for Petrarch)—
she affirms her imaginative commitment to the cultural
significance of desire as an individualizing force:

Come, civil night,
Thou sober-suited matron all in black,
And learn me how to lose a winning match
Played for a pair of stainless maidenhoods.
Hood my unmanned blood, bating in my cheeks,
With thy black mantle till strange love grow bold,
Think true love acted simple modesty.
(3.2.10–16)

Romeo, when he is not drawn by desire deeper and
deeper into Capulet territory, wanders into the open
square where the destinies of the play's other young
men—and in part his own too—are enacted. Because
the young man's deepest loyalty is to his friends, Romeo
is not really asked to choose between Juliet and his
family but between Juliet and Mercutio, who are opposed in the play's thematic structure. Thus one function of Mercutio's anti-Petrarchan skepticism about the

idealization of woman is to offer resistance to the adult heterosexuality heralded by Romeo's union with Juliet, resistance on behalf of the regressive pull of adolescent male bonding—being "one of the guys." This distinction, as we have seen, is in part a question of speaking different discourses. Romeo easily picks up Mercutio's banter, even its sly innuendo against women. Mercutio himself regards Romeo's quickness at repartee as the hopeful sign of a return to a "normal" manly identity incompatible with his ridiculous role as lover:

> Why, is not this better now than groaning for love?
> Now art thou sociable, now art thou Romeo, now
> art thou what thou art, by art as well as by nature.
> For this driveling love is like a great natural that
> runs lolling up and down to hide his bauble in a
> hole.   (2.4.90–95)

Implicit here is a central tenet of traditional misogyny that excessive desire for a woman is effeminizing. For Mercutio it is the effeminate lover in Romeo who refuses shamefully to answer Tybalt's challenge: "O calm, dishonorable, vile submission!" he exclaims furiously (3.1.74). Mercutio's death at Tybalt's hands causes Romeo temporarily to agree, obeying the regressive emotional pull of grief and guilt over his own part in Mercutio's defeat. "Why the devil came you between us?" Mercutio asks. "I was hurt under your arm" (3.1.106–8). Why, we might ask instead, should Mercutio have insisted on answering a challenge addressed only to Romeo? Romeo, however, displaces blame onto Juliet: "Thy beauty hath made me effeminate / And in my temper softened valor's steel" (3.1.119–20).

In terms of narrative structure, the death of Mercutio and Romeo's slaying of Tybalt interrupt the lovers' progress from secret marriage to its consummation, suggesting the incompatibility between romantic individualism and adolescent male bonding. The audience experiences this incompatibility as a sudden movement from comedy to tragedy. Suddenly Friar Lawrence must abandon hopes of using the love of Capulet and Montague as a force for social reintegration. Instead, he must desperately stave off Juliet's marriage to Paris, upon which her father insists, by making her counterfeit death and by subjecting her to entombment. The legal finality of consummated marriage—which was the basis for Friar Lawrence's hopes "to turn your households' rancor to pure love" (2.3.99)—becomes the instrument of tragic design. It is only the Nurse who would allow Juliet to accept Paris as husband; we are asked to judge such a prospect so unthinkable that we then agree imaginatively to Friar Lawrence's ghoulish device.

In terms of the play's symbolic vocabulary, Juliet's preparations to imitate death on the very bed where her sexual maturation from girl- to womanhood occurred confirms ironically her earlier premonition about Romeo: "If he be marrièd, / My grave is like to be my wedding bed" (1.5.148–49). Her brief passage contrasts sharply with those of Shakespeare's comic heroines who move out from the social confinement of daughterhood into a freer, less socially defined space (the woods outside Athens in *A Midsummer Night's Dream*, the Forest of Arden in *As You Like It*). There they can exercise a sanctioned, limited freedom in the romantic experimentation of courtship. Juliet is punished for such experimentation in part because hers is more radical; secret marriage symbolically is as irreversible as "real" death. Her journey thus becomes an internal journey in which her commitment to union with Romeo must face the imaginative challenge of complete, claustrophobic isolation and finally death in the Capulet tomb.

It is possible to see the lovers' story, as some critics

have done, as Shakespeare's dramatic realization of the ruling metaphors of Petrarchan love poetry—particularly its fascination with "death-marked love" (1. Chorus. 9).[3] But, in pondering the implications of Shakespeare's moving his audience to identify with this narrative of initiative, desire, and power, we also do well to remember the psychosocial dynamics of drama. By heightening their powers of identification, drama gives the members of an audience an embodied image of the possible scope and form of their fears and desires. Here we have seen how tragic form operates to contain the complex play of desire/identification. The metaphors of Petrarchan idealization work as part of a complex, ambivalent discourse of woman whose ultimate social function is to encode the felt differences between men and women on which a dominant male power structure is based. Romeo and Juliet find a new discourse of romantic individualism in which Petrarchan idealization conjoins with the mutual avowal of sexual desire. But their union, as we have seen, imperils the traditional relations between males that is founded upon the exchange of women, whether the violent exchange Gregory and Sampson crudely imagine or the normative exchange planned by Capulet and Paris. Juliet, as the daughter whose erotic willfulness activates her father's transformation from concerned to tyrannical parent, is the greater rebel. Thus the secret marriage in which this new language of feeling is contained cannot here be granted the sanction of a comic outcome. When Romeo and Juliet reunite, it is only to see each other, dead, in the dim confines of the Capulet crypt. In this play the autonomy of romantic individualism remains "starcrossed."

---

1. The story of these massive shifts in European sensibility is being told in the ongoing series of volumes

entitled *A History of Private Life,* gen. eds. Philippe Ariès and Georges Duby (Cambridge, Mass., and London: Harvard University Press). For the period most relevant to *Romeo and Juliet,* see vol. 2, *Revelations of the Medieval World* (1988), pp. 509–630.

2. The best extended discussion of the dynamic of the feud is Coppélia Kahn, *Man's Estate: Masculine Identity in Shakespeare* (Berkeley: University of California Press, 1981), pp. 83 ff.

3. Nicholas Brooke, *Shakespeare's Early Tragedies* (London: Methuen, 1968), pp. 82 ff.

Further Reading

Romeo and Juliet

Boose, Lynda E. "The Father and the Bride in Shakespeare." *PMLA* 97 (1982): 325–47.

Boose discusses *Romeo and Juliet* as one of several plays centered on the father-daughter relationship. Shakespeare consistently depicts fathers whose possessive love for their daughters endangers the family unit, disrupting the marriage ceremony in which the father relinquishes his rights over his daughter to her groom.

Brooke, Nicholas. "*Romeo and Juliet*." In *Shakespeare's Early Tragedies*, pp. 80–106. London and New York: Methuen, 1968.

Brooke sees *Romeo and Juliet* as a dramatic evocation of the world of the love sonnet. The tone is "domestic, romantic, comic (not farcical)," but underscored by the darker love-death tradition of the sonnet form. The play explores this sonnet world, regarding both its superiority and inferiority to the world of the everyday.

Charlton, H. B. "Experiment and Interregnum: *Romeo and Juliet, King John, Julius Caesar.*" In *Shakespearean Tragedy*, pp. 49–82. Cambridge: Cambridge University Press, 1948.

For Charlton, *Romeo and Juliet* is an experimental play in both its subject matter and its focus on fate as the primary cause of tragedy. He argues that the feud acts merely as an agent of fate, which brings Romeo and Juliet to an end that, because of their great passion, we applaud. Charlton, however, finds this a "trick" that brings Shakespeare "no nearer to the heart of tragedy."

Gurr, Andrew. "Intertextuality at Windsor." *Shakespeare Quarterly* 38 (1987): 189–200.

Between May 1594 and 1600, according to Gurr, there were only two companies competing for the attention of London playgoers. This situation led the two companies to become deeply imitative of one another. Gurr traces out some of the influences that *Romeo and Juliet*—an enormous success for Shakespeare's company—had on the plays of his rivals.

Kahn, Coppélia. "Coming of Age: Marriage and Manhood in *Romeo and Juliet* and *The Taming of the Shrew.*" In *Man's Estate: Masculine Identity in Shakespeare*, pp. 82–118. Berkeley: University of California Press, 1981.

For Kahn, *Romeo and Juliet* enacts a conflict between differing conceptions of manhood: on the one hand, manhood as "violence on behalf of the fathers" and, on the other, "manhood as separation from the fathers and sexual union with women." The feud, therefore, is a deadly rite of passage that "promotes masculinity at the price of life." Romeo and Juliet's attempt to create and preserve identities outside the violence of the feud is ultimately doomed, and their union can be achieved only in death.

Laslett, Peter. *The World We Have Lost—Further Explored*. London: Methuen, 1983.

Laslett's study of the social structure of preindustrial England reveals misbeliefs about the age of marriage and childbearing in Shakespeare's time. Marriage at the age of fourteen—Juliet's age—would have been very rare in Elizabethan and Jacobean England. Juliet's early marriage, and that of her mother, who claims to have been a mother at Juliet's age, would have been very far removed from the average experience of the audience.

Lawlor, John. *"Romeo and Juliet."* In *Early Shakespeare,* edited by John Russell Brown and Bernard Harris, pp. 123–44. Stratford-upon-Avon Studies 3. London: Edward Arnold, 1961.

Lawlor considers the medieval conception of tragedy and Shakespeare's tragic plays written before *Romeo and Juliet* to account for the play's alleged shortcomings. According to Lawlor, Shakespeare rejects the stereotype of "man as merely the weak subject of heaven's stratagems" and reinvests medieval tragedy with a sense of greater good. For Lawlor, this makes *Romeo and Juliet* "profoundly consistent" with Shakespeare's other great tragedies.

Novy, Marianne. "Violence, Love, and Gender in *Romeo and Juliet* and *Troilus and Cressida.*" In *Love's Argument: Gender Relations in Shakespeare,* pp. 99–124. Chapel Hill: University of North Carolina Press, 1984.

Novy describes Romeo and Juliet's love as a challenge to Verona's associations of masculinity and sexuality with violence. The protagonists' secrecy about their relationship is in part due to their awareness of these violently distorted conceptions of manhood and sexual relations. Romeo and Juliet's failure ultimately to transcend the gender definitions of Verona makes "disaster inevitable."

Porter, Henry. *The Mad Women of Abingdon,* edited by Marianne Brish Evett. New York: Garland, 1980.

Porter's play parallels *Romeo and Juliet* both verbally and in its "balcony scene." The family feud between Mistress Barnes and Mistress Goursey has led some critics to regard the play as a gentle spoof of *Romeo and Juliet.* Other critics, however, date the play as early as 1588 and claim that Porter's work was a source for Shakespeare.

Porter, Joseph A. *Shakespeare's Mercutio: His History and Drama.* Chapel Hill: University of North Carolina Press, 1988.

In an attempt to account for Mercutio's ability to discomfit readers across four centuries, Porter traces the history of Mercutio before Shakespeare (in his evolution from the Greek Hermes, to the Roman Mercurius, to the Renaissance Mercury), with Shakespeare, and after Shakespeare. Porter also examines Shakespeare's representation of the conflict between male friendship and married love as it is played out in the Mercutio-Romeo-Juliet triangle.

Shakespeare, William. *The Most Excellent and Lamentable Tragedie of Romeo and Juliet,* edited by George W. Williams. Durham: Duke University Press, 1964.

Following a brief summary of bibliographical theories concerning the early printed texts of *Romeo and Juliet,* Williams provides an edition based upon the second quarto (Q2, 1599) of Shakespeare's play. Although Q2 cannot be said "without qualification" to be based upon Shakespeare's manuscript throughout, Q2 is accepted by Williams as the edition of "prime authority."

Snyder, Susan. "Beyond Comedy: *Romeo and Juliet* and *Othello.*" In *The Comic Matrix of Shakespeare's Tragedies,* pp. 56–90. Princeton: Princeton University Press, 1979.

Up until Mercutio's death in Act 3, Snyder contends, *Romeo and Juliet* is essentially a comedy. With his death, however, the play reverses its comic movement and heads toward tragedy. This process of becoming rather than simply being tragic makes *Romeo and Juliet* unique among Shakespeare's tragedies.

Stone, Lawrence. *The Family, Sex and Marriage in England 1500–1800.* New York: Harper & Row, 1977.

Stone's massive study sheds interesting light on *Romeo and Juliet*'s depiction of marriage in a patriarchal society. According to Stone, the ideal of a "companionate" marriage increasingly surmounted the patriarchal model of marriage in the sixteenth and seventeenth centuries.

Utterback, Raymond V. "The Death of Mercutio." *Shakespeare Quarterly* 24 (1973): 105–16.

Reading Mercutio's death as a primary motivating force for the major subsequent events, Utterback contends that the death establishes a pattern that runs throughout the play. This pattern, comprising threats, anxieties, dangers, and risks, provides a background of constant tension against which the characters move. Mercutio's death, therefore, introduces "the forces and patterns of dramatic action" that lead to the ultimate tragedy.

Whittier, Gayle. "The Sonnet's Body and the Body Sonnetized." *Shakespeare Quarterly* 40 (1989): 27–41.

Whittier describes *Romeo and Juliet*'s inheritance of the Petrarchan convention as one "emptied of its traditional lyric treasures." Petrarch's influential sonnet form does operate in the play, but more as a structuring feature than a verbal one. According to Whittier, Shakespeare has transformed the conventions of Petrarchan poetry so that "lyric freedom" has declined to "tragic fact."

Shakespeare's Language

Abbott, E. A. *A Shakespearian Grammar.* New York: Haskell House, 1972.

This compact reference book, first published in 1870,

helps with many difficulties in Shakespeare's language. It systematically accounts for a host of differences between Shakespeare's usage and sentence structure and our own.

Blake, Norman. *Shakespeare's Language: An Introduction.* New York: St. Martin's Press, 1983.

This general introduction to Elizabethan English discusses various aspects of the language of Shakespeare and his contemporaries, offering possible meanings for hundreds of ambiguous constructions.

Dobson, E. J. *English Pronunciation, 1500–1700.* 2 vols. Oxford: Clarendon Press, 1968.

This long and technical work includes chapters on spelling (and its reformation), phonetics, stressed vowels, and consonants in early modern English.

Houston, John. *Shakespearean Sentences: A Study in Style and Syntax.* Baton Rouge: Louisiana State University Press, 1988.

Houston studies Shakespeare's stylistic choices, considering matters such as sentence length and the relative positions of subject, verb, and direct object. Examining plays throughout the canon in a roughly chronological, developmental order, he analyzes how sentence structure is used in setting tone, in characterization, and for other dramatic purposes.

Onions, C. T. *A Shakespeare Glossary.* Oxford: Clarendon Press, 1986.

This revised edition updates Onions's standard, selective glossary of words and phrases in Shakespeare's plays that are now obsolete, archaic, or obscure.

Partridge, Eric. *Shakespeare's Bawdy.* London: Routledge & Kegan Paul, 1955.

After an introductory essay, "The Sexual, the Homo-
sexual, and Non-Sexual Bawdy in Shakespeare," Partridge provides a comprehensive glossary of "bawdy"
phrases and words from the plays.

Robinson, Randal. *Unlocking Shakespeare's Language:
Help for the Teacher and Student.* Urbana, Ill.: National
Council of Teachers of English and the ERIC Clearing-
house on Reading and Communication Skills, 1989.

Specifically designed for the high-school and under-
graduate college teacher and student, Robinson's book
addresses the problems that most often hinder present-
day readers of Shakespeare. Through work with his own
students, Robinson found that many readers today are
particularly puzzled by such stylistic characteristics as
subject-verb inversion, interrupted structures, and com-
pression. He shows how our own colloquial language
contains comparable structures, and thus helps students
recognize such structures when they find them in
Shakespeare's plays. This book supplies worksheets—
with examples from major plays—to illuminate and
remedy such problems as unusual sequences of words
and the separation of related parts of sentences.

Shakespeare's Life

Baldwin, T. W. *William Shakspere's Petty School.* Urbana:
University of Illinois Press, 1943.

Baldwin here investigates the theory and practice of
the petty school, the first level of education in Elizabethan England. He focuses on that educational system
primarily as it is reflected in Shakespeare's art.

Baldwin, T. W. *William Shakspere's Small Latine and
Lesse Greeke.* 2 vols. Urbana: University of Illinois Press,
1944.

Baldwin attacks the view that Shakespeare was an uneducated genius—a view that had been dominant among Shakespeareans since the eighteenth century. Instead, Baldwin shows, the educational system of Shakespeare's time would have given the playwright a strong background in the classics, and there is much in the plays that shows how Shakespeare benefited from such an education.

Beier, A. L., and Roger Finlay, eds. *London 1500–1700: The Making of the Metropolis.* New York: Longman, 1986.

Focusing on the economic and social history of early modern London, these collected essays probe aspects of metropolitan life, including "Population and Disease," "Commerce and Manufacture," and "Society and Change."

Bentley, G. E. *Shakespeare's Life: A Biographical Handbook.* New Haven: Yale University Press, 1961.

This "just-the-facts" account presents the surviving documents of Shakespeare's life against an Elizabethan background.

Chambers, E. K. *William Shakespeare: A Study of Facts and Problems.* 2 vols. Oxford: Clarendon Press, 1930.

Analyzing in great detail the scant historical data, Chambers's complex, scholarly study considers the nature of the texts in which Shakespeare's work is preserved.

Cressy, David. *Education in Tudor and Stuart England.* London: Edward Arnold, 1975.

This volume collects sixteenth-, seventeenth-, and early eighteenth-century documents detailing aspects of formal education in England, such as the curriculum, the control and organization of education, and the education of women.

Dutton, Richard. *William Shakespeare: A Literary Life.* New York: St. Martin's Press, 1989.

Not a biography in the traditional sense, Dutton's very readable work nevertheless "follows the contours of Shakespeare's life" as he examines Shakespeare's career as playwright and poet, with consideration of his patrons, theatrical associations, and audience.

Fraser, Russell. *Young Shakespeare.* New York: Columbia University Press, 1988.

Fraser focuses on Shakespeare's first thirty years, paying attention simultaneously to his life and art.

De Grazia, Margreta. *Shakespeare Verbatim: The Reproduction of Authenticity and the Apparatus of 1790.* Oxford: Clarendon Press, 1991.

De Grazia traces and discusses the development of such editorial criteria as authenticity, historical periodization, factual biography, chronological developments, and close reading, locating as the point of origin Edmond Malone's 1790 edition of Shakespeare's works. There are interesting chapters on the First Folio and on the "legendary" versus the "documented" Shakespeare.

Schoenbaum, S. *William Shakespeare: A Compact Documentary Life.* New York: Oxford University Press, 1977.

This standard biography economically presents the essential documents from Shakespeare's time in an accessible narrative account of the playwright's life.

Shakespeare's Theater

Bentley, G. E. *The Profession of Player in Shakespeare's Time, 1590–1642.* Princeton: Princeton University Press, 1984.

Bentley readably sets forth a wealth of evidence about performance in Shakespeare's time, with special attention to the relations between player and company, and the business of casting, managing, and touring.

Berry, Herbert. *Shakespeare's Playhouses.* New York: AMS Press, 1987.

Berry's six essays collected here discuss (with illustrations) varying aspects of the four playhouses in which Shakespeare had a financial stake: the Theatre in Shoreditch, the Blackfriars, and the first and second Globe.

Cook, Ann Jennalie. *The Privileged Playgoers of Shakespeare's London.* Princeton: Princeton University Press, 1981.

Cook's work argues, on the basis of sociological, economic, and documentary evidence, that Shakespeare's audience—and the audience for English Renaissance drama generally—consisted mainly of the "privileged."

Greg, W. W. *Dramatic Documents from the Elizabethan Playhouses.* 2 vols. Oxford: Clarendon Press, 1931.

Greg itemizes and briefly describes almost all the play manuscripts that survive from the period 1590 to around 1660, including, among other things, players' parts. His second volume offers facsimiles of selected manuscripts.

Gurr, Andrew. *Playgoing in Shakespeare's London.* Cambridge: Cambridge University Press, 1987.

Gurr charts how the theatrical enterprise developed from its modest beginnings in the 1560s to become a thriving institution in the 1600s. He argues that there were important changes over the period 1567–1644 in the playhouses, the audience, and the plays.

Harbage, Alfred. *Shakespeare's Audience.* New York: Columbia University Press, 1941.
Harbage investigates the fragmentary surviving evidence to interpret the size, composition, and behavior of Shakespeare's audience.

Hattaway, Michael. *Elizabethan Popular Theatre: Plays in Performance.* London: Routledge & Kegan Paul, 1982.
Beginning with a study of the popular drama of the late Elizabethan age—a description of the stages, performance conditions, and acting of the period—this volume concludes with an analysis of five well-known plays of the 1590s, one of them (*Titus Andronicus*) by Shakespeare.

Shapiro, Michael. *Children of the Revels: The Boy Companies of Shakespeare's Time and Their Plays.* New York: Columbia University Press, 1977.
Shapiro chronicles the history of the amateur and quasi-professional child companies that flourished in London at the end of Elizabeth's reign and the beginning of James's.

The Publication of Shakespeare's Plays

Blayney, Peter. *The First Folio of Shakespeare.* Hanover, Md.: Folger, 1991.
Blayney's accessible account of the printing and later life of the First Folio—an amply illustrated catalogue to

a 1991 Folger Shakespeare Library exhibition—analyzes the mechanical production of the First Folio, describing how the Folio was made, by whom and for whom, how much it cost, and its ups and downs (or, rather, downs and ups) since its printing in 1623.

Hinman, Charlton. *The Printing and Proof-Reading of the First Folio of Shakespeare*. 2 vols. Oxford: Clarendon Press, 1963.

In the most arduous study of a single book ever undertaken, Hinman attempts to reconstruct how the Shakespeare First Folio of 1623 was set into type and run off the press, sheet by sheet. He also provides almost all the known variations in readings from copy to copy.

Hinman, Charlton. *The Norton Facsimile: The First Folio of Shakespeare*. New York: W. W. Norton, 1968.

This facsimile presents a photographic reproduction of an "ideal" copy of the First Folio of Shakespeare; Hinman attempts to represent each page in its most fully corrected state.

Key to
Famous Lines and Phrases

A pair of star-crossed lovers . . .   [*Chorus*—Pro. 6]

. . . sad hours seem long.   [*Romeo*—1.1.166]

Alas that love, so gentle in his view,
Should be so tyrannous and rough in proof!
    [*Benvolio*—1.1.174–75]

. . . I will make thee think thy swan a crow.
    [*Benvolio*—1.2.94]

. . . Queen Mab . . . She is the fairies' midwife . . .
    [*Mercutio*—1.4.58–59]

O, she doth teach the torches to burn bright!
It seems she hangs upon the cheek of night
Like a rich jewel in an Ethiop's ear . . .
    [*Romeo*—1.5.51–53]

You kiss by th' book.   [*Juliet*—1.5.122]

My only love sprung from my only hate!
Too early seen unknown, and known too late!
    [*Juliet*—1.5.152–53]

He jests at scars that never felt a wound.
But soft, what light through yonder window breaks?
    [*Romeo*—2.2.1–2]

O Romeo, Romeo, wherefore art thou Romeo?
    [*Juliet*—2.2.36]

279

That which we call a rose
By any other word would smell as sweet.

[*Juliet*—2.2.46–47]

O, swear not by the moon, th' inconstant moon,
That monthly changes in her circled orb,
Lest that thy love prove likewise variable.

[*Juliet*—2.2.114–16]

Love goes toward love as schoolboys from their books,
But love from love, toward school with heavy looks.

[*Romeo*—2.2.166–68]

How silver-sweet sound lovers' tongues by night,
Like softest music to attending ears.

[*Romeo*—2.2.176–77]

Good night, good night. Parting is such sweet sorrow
That I shall say "Good night" till it be morrow.

[*Juliet*—2.2.199–201]

Thy head is as full of quarrels as an egg is full of
meat . . .   [*Mercutio*—3.1.23–24]

. . . 'tis not so deep as a well, nor so wide as a church
door, but 'tis enough. 'Twill serve.

[*Mercutio*—3.1.100–1]

A plague o' both your houses!   [*Mercutio*—3.1.111]

Gallop apace, you fiery-footed steeds . . . [*Juliet*—3.2.1]

Wilt thou be gone? It is not yet near day.
It was the nightingale, and not the lark,
That pierced the fearful hollow of thine ear.

[*Juliet*—3.5.1–3]

Night's candles are burnt out, and jocund day
Stands tiptoe on the misty mountain-tops.

[*Romeo*—3.5.9–10]

Thank me no thankings, nor proud me no prouds . . .

[*Capulet*—3.5.157]

. . . past hope, past care, past help.   [*Juliet*—4.1.46]

Not stepping o'er the bounds of modesty.

[*Juliet*—4.2.28]

Death, that hath sucked the honey of thy breath,
Hath had no power yet upon thy beauty.

[*Romeo*—5.3.92–93]

. . . never was a story of more woe
Than this of Juliet and her Romeo.

[*Prince*—5.3.320–21]